BEYOND PRODUCT

BEYOND PRODUCT

How Exceptional Founders

Embrace Marketing to Create and

Capture Value for their Business

JILL SOLEY
TODD WILMS

NEW YORK

LONDON • NASHVILLE • MELBOURNE • VANCOUVER

BEYOND PRODUCT

How Exceptional Founders Embrace Marketing to Create and Capture
Value for Their Business

Published in New York, New York, by Morgan James Publishing. Morgan James is a
trademark of Morgan James, LLC. www.MorganJamesPublishing.com

ISBN 9781642791259 paperback
ISBN 9781642791266 eBook
Library of Congress Control Number: 2018906784

Interior Design by:
Christopher Kirk
www.GFSstudio.com

Morgan James is a proud partner of Habitat for Humanity Peninsula
and Greater Williamsburg. Partners in building since 2006.

Get involved today! Visit
MorganJamesPublishing.com/giving-back

DEDICATION

To Erin
The Boys
Mom and Dad
You made all things possible!

To Cam, my love, my partner, and my rock.
My parents, who taught me to look beyond the horizon.
And, of course, my boys. You light up my world!
Believe in yourself. Always.

CONTENTS

1
INTRODUCTION

CoTap was a work texting product launched by experienced ex-Yammer product and engineering executives. Their go-to-market strategy was freemium, which had worked for Yammer and seemed like a good idea. But CoTap "didn't really fly off the shelves." Eventually the leadership found itself at a crossroads, realizing, "Wow, we really built a pretty cool core messaging app. But we don't really know the best way to take it to market."

They eventually brought in Stacey Epstein, a successful CMO, as their new CEO because "this was not an engineering problem that needed to be solved, nor a product problem. This was all about go-to-market."

Stacey narrowed the target market to one where Slack is not, added a bunch of features to the core CoTap texting product, and then rebranded to Zinc, changed freemium to a free trial, and infused new growth into the company.

E ach year, 600,000 companies start up in the US. More than three-quarters of those fail.

Over half of those failures—250,000 companies—cite lack of market need or poor marketing as the cause.[1]

How does that happen? Early on in the life of a startup, founders focus heavily on their product, as they should. The product is critically important and central to the business. But it isn't enough. To be successful, you need to build a business, not just a product. Having the best product won't matter if no one knows about it or why it should matter to them. Understanding marketing and how to go to market successfully will make or break your business.

We know that building and growing a business is hard. If you are like the founders we have worked with and interviewed for this book, you see some unique opportunity or feel compelled to solve some problem in the world.

Even for those who manage to bring their product to life, finding customers and then getting them to buy and use the product can be more challenging than many realize.

We can't solve all of your problems, but we know how to take your product to market. And we've brought in 50 additional business leaders to advise you on how to grow your business from that basic idea up through to your eventual exit.

---

1   Heather Long, "Where Are All the Startups? US Entrepreneurship Near a 40-Year Low," CNN. com, September 8, 2016, https://money.cnn.com/2016/09/08/news/economy/us-startups-near-40-year-low/index.html; "Entrepreneurship and the US Economy," US Bureau of Labor Statistics, April 28, 2016, https://www.bls.gov/bdm/entrepreneurship/entrepreneurship.htm; Patrick Henry, "Why Some Startups Succeed (and Most Fail), Entrepreneur.com, February 18, 2017, https://www.entrepreneur.com/article/288769; https://www.cbinsights.com/research/startup-failure-reasons-top.

Not long ago, Jill had coffee with a founder/CEO. They'd been chatting for a while when he confided, "My company is at a point where I think we need marketing. But, I don't really know what it is or where to start. Can you help?"

Even founders who do have marketing knowledge struggle to determine when and how to properly engage in—and extract the most from—marketing. And even some founders who are marketers by background have claimed to struggle to do it well, simply because they are stretched in so many directions.

Apostrophe co-founder and CEO Cheryl Kellond put it well:

> I'm the co-founder that can market. And I'm doing so many other things that on the marketing side, I might as well be a junior-level marketer. I feel like I'm flailing around like a child. I'm just about to bring in a head of marketing, and it's been so refreshing talking to the right candidates because it's reminding me how it's supposed to be done.

Dale Sakai, a successful CEO, strategic planning expert, and co-founder of the startup Obo, put it this way:

> If you look back at different industries, the company that has ended up in the top slot with the most market share is generally not the company with the best technology, but the one that had the best marketing.

Marketing is critical to success, yet many founders and leaders are skeptical and hesitant about it. There are several common reasons for this resistance:

- **Prior bad experience:** Some founders have had bad experiences with marketers and are hesitant to waste their time, effort, and energy—as well as their trust—on repeating a similar experience. Just like some founders aren't great founders, some marketers aren't great marketers. Sometimes it is a case of poor marketing. Other times it is the product of misaligned expectations. Either way, bad memories can be hard to overcome.

- **Lack of understanding:** Most people—even most marketers—have a difficult time defining what marketing is and how best to use it. So it is not surprising that many founders struggle with marketing, especially if they think of it in a limited or ineffective way.
- **Communication issues:** ABM, CPL, TOFU, CRO, DM… Marketers tend to use jargon, inside baseball language, and three letter acronyms (or TLAs—with no lack of irony) more than anyone. This makes understanding and communicating with marketing challenging at times.
- **Product mythology:** Many believe that if they build it, the customers will come, that the better mousetrap will lead the world to your door. But many "best in class" products fail. Even if the better product would win, you can get there easier, faster, cheaper with great marketing.
- **It can happen later:** Many believe that marketing is something to do later, a problem to address down the road. As this book will illustrate, marketing is something that starts as the twin of your idea. The two—product and marketing—go hand in hand, and one should not exist without the other.

Marketing will significantly increase your chances of success, and it can act as a multiplier for sales, if you understand what it is and know how to use it.

This book is designed to be a source for better understanding marketing, knowing how and when to use marketing, and how to find the talented employees and partners to help you succeed with your idea. We will walk you through how to best use these insights and, even more importantly, when to use them.

Why This Book

We wrote this book because we worked with many amazing founders and saw firsthand their drive and passion to pursue what they believe in and the desire to change the world. It has been a daily inspiration for us both throughout our careers and in the writing of this book.

Startup founders have a tremendous weight upon their shoulders. You are the first "everything" for your idea—first evangelist and salesperson, first customer service person, first finance person, first operations person, and yes, first marketer. Everyone you bring on board looks to you for answers, even when the answers aren't there.

Everyone needs a little help, so this book was crafted to give founders insights, guidance, strategies, and practical advice to help them answer some of those tough questions, make even smarter decisions, and know where and how to get the help needed as they evolve their idea.

We define marketing in the next chapter and describe how the focus of marketing will shift over time. Many of the core marketing challenges you are likely to face are related to product/market fit. *A great product that doesn't know where it fits in the marketplace, who the buyer is, why they buy, how to reach them, where to reach them, when to reach them, or how often to reach them is destined to fail.*

That is all marketing.

Who We Are

We, Todd and Jill, have many years of career experience between us, including a wealth of both startup and brand name experiences. We've faced all manner of successes and failures, and learned from amazing mentors and colleagues at companies like Freshworks, Adobe, Siebel, SAP, and PayPal, many others you've never heard of, and some that no longer exist.

Over our careers, we've been advisors on seed rounds, helped organizations climb through multiple rounds of funding, launched new products and sunset old ones, transformed stagnant mature businesses into new growth engines, expanded businesses into new markets around the globe, and endured both long-lasting as well as challenging relationships with founders.

We interviewed more than 50 business leaders and subject matter experts in the making of this book. These are successful entrepreneurs, investors, marketers, and advisors who all know their craft really well. Many are not household names or the storied Silicon Valley unicorns we hear about. But they are people who live and breathe their craft and have lived through what you are likely experiencing right now. We have gained insights from each and every one of these conversations and have synthesized these stories into a simple framework to guide your marketing journey.

Who This Book Is For

This book is intended for entrepreneurs, particularly tech startup founders. We address you and talk directly to you. You may be bootstrapping a new venture or launching a skunkworks project within a large enterprise or part of a more formal incubator program. Some of you are doing this for the very first time, while others may have five other businesses under your belts. Some are still in the early concepting phases, and some are much further along.

We therefore cover both basic and advanced ideas. We assume a basic understanding of how to grow a business, but we explain a few things that the veteran will have learned along their journey. We don't want to talk down to anyone, but we aspire to leave no one behind. This book also includes information that will be useful no matter what kind of startup, but you'll find that the majority of our examples come from business-to-business tech startups.

Investors, advisors, team members, and other stakeholders, including marketing, will benefit from this book. While the initial business idea may not be yours, you are playing a key role—financial or otherwise. It is your job to partner with your founders and CEOs and help them on the journey to build an amazing business. We hope this book serves as a conversation starter and can help your collaboration. You are part of the story.

How to Read This Book

Every entrepreneur is different. You are in a unique place in your journey to create a successful business. Even your definition of "successful" will be unique to you. This book has been structured to help you find what you need when you need it.

The book has been designed to be able to be read in one sitting. Most leaders don't have time for a Tolstoyan epic or a textbook. Our goal is to give you the relevant information in a relatively short period of time. This is a book that will evolve with your business—as your idea grows and your business comes up against new challenges, specific chapters will take on new meaning as you look for ways to leverage marketing.

This book will provide a primer on "What is marketing?" and walk you through the five phases of an organization's growth. These phases are not organized by funding or revenue, but rather by the phases of startup growth:

1. Prove the **Idea**
2. Prove the **Product**
3. Prove the **Business**
4. **Grow** the Business
5. **Exit** the Business

Each chapter follows a similar pattern to help you navigate where you are at any given time and the key challenges to focus on next. You may find you fit perfectly in a certain phase, or you may see that you are a little bit of a blend of two phases. Of course real life doesn't happen so neatly, and these stages will overlap. But this framework will provide a structure to think about your startup's growth and how to approach marketing at each phase.

Because each phase is meant to be a standalone chapter, some ideas are repeated across multiple chapters, especially when they are particularly relevant to that topic. We want founders to be able to read it in full, and then revisit each chapter as needed without having to start from scratch again.

Even if you aren't starting a new venture today, we found from our conversations that most founders would have benefitted from having these insights when they first started crafting the plans for their organization. Don't think you need to have accomplished specific milestones to start thinking about how you are going to promote your idea. Making smart decisions from the very beginning will save you time, energy, and money.

This project has been crafted for the entire life of your business. From that first idea and all the way through your exit, we offer perspectives and resources to help you through those stages. None of this is perfectly black and white, but each chapter covers a set of challenges typical to that stage of growth and provides a path to address them.

We wish you every success on your journey and hope these insights help you in some way as you take your big idea and turn it into a big success.

Todd Nilms AND Phil Bley

2
WHAT IS MARKETING?

Who cares what marketing is?

Really. Who cares?

As a founder, you need to worry about payroll, getting your next round of funding, securing office space, hiring key employees, keeping your board happy, bringing in customers, and making sure your customers stay happy.

What difference does it make what exactly marketing is? What you need are answers—plain and simple answers to these and all your other challenges.

This chapter will give you a working understanding of the role that marketing plays and will help you define the organization and structure. This will be important when you start building your team and need to know how to find the right person and what the heck the person across the table is saying to you.

There is a famous parable that has been adopted by business leaders around the world:

A group of blind men heard that a strange animal called an elephant had been brought to the town, but none of them were aware of its shape and form. Out of curiosity, they said: "We must inspect and learn to know it by touch." Soon, they found the elephant and approached it. The first person's hand landed on the trunk, and he said, "It is like a thick snake." The second's hand reached its ear, which seemed like a kind of fan. Another person touched its leg and said that the elephant like a pillar or tree trunk. Others claimed the elephant was like "a wall," "a rope," or "a spear."

The parable illustrates that each person sees the world differently through their particular perspective and experiences. This is very true with marketing. For some it is a lead-generating engine, for others it is the website, a few may see it as a brand exercise, and yet others see it as just a big expense or "a necessary evil."

Confusion about what exactly marketing is drives the majority of the problems founders face with it. In our 30+ years of combined experience, the definition has shifted and evolved, and even some experts disagree on what marketing is. No wonder there is confusion.

The definition we like best is that marketing is the bridge between product and sales (and other customer-facing functions) and the customer. And no, that doesn't mean that other functions aren't allowed to talk to customers. It means that marketing connects the product to the marketplace, helping the organization understand exactly who their customer really is and what they want and helping the customer understand what the product is and how it can benefit them. Marketing helps sales by attracting prospective customers, making sure they are aware of the product, and generating interest. Marketing also helps sales understand how to communicate with those customers and provides content and tools to help sales teams educate buyers and drive purchases. In essence it helps the organization know what to sell and to whom and how. In this light, marketing is the organization that first connects but then later facilitates and helps those groups communicate. Generating leads can be a part of it, just like creating product demonstrations or case studies or even blog posts, but seeing only these aspects of marketing is like touching the tail of the elephant—it misses the bigger picture.

Marketing is there for the two-way communication between those key internal groups in your organization and the external customer. The idea of two-way communication is important, because marketing should not just be a megaphone to make your message louder. Marketing should help the business know how customers are reacting to products, messaging, and new market trends. Marketing should have a wealth of data and insights in front of them (even without conducting "official" research)—this information is a natural result of every program that they run. They can see much of it happen before them. The communication may be a piece of statistical analysis—a change in market share, or another number going up or down—but that communication informs product and sales and leadership what is happening and, hopefully, why.

Where we have often seen the struggle is when (1) the marketing team is operating in "broadcast mode," talking *at* the customers with the idea that if the business talks loud enough or often enough the customer will buy; (2) the marketing communication, outreach, and experiences are uncoordinated and inconsistent, confusing the prospects and customers; or (3) the founder, likely from some previous bad experience, mistrusts or misunderstands marketing and—whether intended or not—puts limits on marketing that prevent success.

Jon Miller, CEO and Founder of Engagio and Co-founder of Marketo, on "What Is Marketing?"
To create awareness and preference at every stage of the buyer's journey.

Some of the confusion around the role of marketing is due to this overlap with these other functions. In consumer businesses, in fact, user acquisition and conversion are so intricately tied to the product itself that while there may be separate teams focused on branding and advertising, product marketing is often part of the product manager function. In B2B or business-focused companies, a separate product marketing team generally handles messaging, positioning, pricing, and other aspects of going to market. This team may report into the head of product and should have objectives that are closely aligned with those of the product team and the overall business objectives.

Just as the product team builds product and the sales team sells, the marketing organization should market. It should promote the organization and its products or services. It should get the word out. It should help the product team know what customers want. It should help sales sell better, faster, and more. If done right, marketing should be a multiplier for sales. And marketing should have clear, measurable goals and be held accountable for revenue.

Marketing teams may be tasked with building awareness, negating a crisis, helping with a specific set of customers, or other non-near-term revenue objectives. Even these efforts can be tied to growth; it may simply be in terms of customer lifetime value or it may be a matter of connecting the dots between content created or a program run and customer purchases. The key is that marketing should be held accountable for growth.

Now let's extend that idea of the customer as the entire marketplace and call them your audience. Besides your customers, investors, board members, advisors, mentors, friends of the company, analysts, influencers, partners, press and media, and social media can make this even more complicated. Marketing should play a critical role in helping those strategic relationships as well, and they don't all care about the same things.

Bill Macaitis, Former CMO of Slack and Zendesk, on "What Is Marketing?"
How you define marketing impacts people's perceptions of what the role is. Many in B2B believe marketing's role is to get leads in the door and hand them off to sales…I respond negatively to that…Marketing has a role to shepherd the journey of a prospect through their entire buying experience and through their journey as a customer…Marketing has some of the best tools to listen to understand to support and nurture that journey and be an advocate for the whole customer experience…

Ultimately, marketing's role is to help spread the word, increase growth, and give prospects and customers an amazing experience. The bar is to get people to recommend you, not just to buy your product…All the fundamentals—your CAC payback, your magic number—work better when you have a healthy growth rate that comes from organic word of mouth.

As a founder, you are the first marketing person, that very first chief marketing officer (CMO), if you will. Those first pitches that persuade initial investors, employees, and customers; sizing up your market; aligning your product with that market; and positioning your product or service offering to that market—all are marketing.

We spoke to one successful founder who proclaimed—in no uncertain terms—that he grew the business to a successful acquisition (and later IPO) without any marketing. He didn't need it. They focused on building a great service and then sold it. Word of mouth propelled them to success. They did some lead generation work at later stages, but they had true organic growth without any marketing.

When walked through the chapters and major tenets of this book, he recognized that he did, in fact, do marketing. He just didn't think of those activities as marketing.

As this founder dug deeper and looked at what he had done through the lens of our framework, he saw that he was actually doing marketing all along. The founder's thought leadership, speaking at events, and their creation of a publicized "state of the marketplace" were fantastic examples of content, brand marketing, and PR.

This founder ran a highly successful business to a great IPO and has stayed on to evolve it even further. Even really talented founders get this wrong or just don't have the time to spend on it and make assumptions. Those assumptions may not even be conscious, or they may be made from a prior bad experience with marketing. But conscious or not, chosen or not, they will cause your organization a major problem: without that two-way connection between your customers (and all your audiences) and your organization, your path to success will be harder, slower, and ultimately more costly. And you will never fully know what could have been in store for you if you had had a great marketing strategy and a team to execute it.

Marketing is a discipline like any other in your organization. It can be lean and mean, or fat and bloated. It can be too much too soon, or not enough too late. What the following chapters are designed to do is help you find the best path forward with marketing by your side. This means the right talent, the right tech, and the right strategy—all at the right time.

Accenture published a study in December 2017 stating that 41% of consumers surveyed switched brands because of lack of trust and lack of a personalized experience—knowing who your customer is and creating products and experiences for them—costing US businesses $756 billion.[2]

If You Build It, They Won't Come

Dale Sakai on "What Is Marketing?"
Fundamentally, marketing is about understanding the marketplace, what the

---

2   David Kirkpatrick, "Accenture: Lack of Personalization, Consumer Trust Cost Businesses $756B Last Year," Marketing Dive, December 11, 2017, https://www.marketingdive.com/news/accenture-lack-of-personalization-consumer-trust-cost-businesses-756b-la/512693.

market wants, and what your target segment really wants, and then building an offering to meet that market... That's pretty commonsense. Build a product that people want as opposed to building a product and then figuring out if somebody wants it. Usually that doesn't work well...

There is a popular belief that if you build a great product or service, it will sell itself. We have heard a few unicorns (startups valued at over $1 billion, like Uber or Facebook) tout this idea that marketing wasn't necessary to their growth. What they are really saying is, "We did what we did without a CMO, a marketing team, ad campaigns, or a focus on lead generation."

There are always exceptions, but even those exceptions are increasingly exceptional. There is so much noise in the marketplace, and it is becoming even more crowded, so simply building the perfect mousetrap is not enough. This can be hard to hear or acknowledge for a founder. As a founder, your product is akin to your child. That level of rejection by a market that doesn't immediately connect with your idea can feel personal.

Paul Greenberg of the The 56Group, an author and contributor on ZDNet, put it this way:

> Companies submit a questionnaire for the CRM Watchlist, one that consists of a series of very detailed questions to describe their business. I will always penalize them if they describe themselves as the "only XYZ in the market today." That is just patently false, and I would challenge someone to try to prove that. You may do something better or in a more unique way, but rare is the truly and fully original product. In fact, if "we are the only company who" isn't followed by their description of the creation of a new element for the periodic table, then it's pretty likely they aren't the only company doing what they claim.

A great product can do much of the heavy lifting to connect to your audience and can make marketing that product easier. But marketing can and should make this easier, faster, and cheaper—yes, all three. It doesn't matter how great your product is if no one knows or no one understands how it can help them.

The old saying goes: "He who has a thing to sell and goes and whispers in a well is not so apt to get the dollars as he who climbs a tree and hollers." Now, why you would whisper into a well is beyond us, but that saying still holds true—a great product without marketing can't hold a candle to a great one with it.

We would even make the point one step further: a great product without marketing can't hold a candle to a good one with great marketing.

Does Starbucks really have the best coffee?

Is Red Bull really the best energy drink?

Is Apple really the best at innovation?

Now think about the brands you know and love. Food, leisure, automotive, sports, business technology, whatever. Are they amazing products that you admire and use? How did you learn about them? What drew you to them?

Build a great product and share your vision of what it can be with the world. Then use marketing to create a connection between your customer (and audiences) and your organization so that people can find, interact with, and buy your amazing product.

The Five Components of Marketing

For many founders, the roles within marketing can be confusing. At your early stages, there may be just one person who does all of these as best they can, likely with a focus on one or two in particular. But as the organization grows, these roles and people are likely to form into organizations within the marketing function.

What is often daunting for early founders is the thought that you might have to create a large (read: expensive) marketing organization to be effective. This book will help you assess who you actually need to hire at each phase of your startup's growth.

It is also critically important to understand that there is no one perfect structure for the marketing organization. Many of the decisions you make will be based on individual people and their abilities and the specifics of your business.

As your people play multiple roles in your earlier stages, you may find that the roles don't fit into neat categories. For instance, your operations person may be a great blogger, so content resides in the operations group for a time. That is perfectly fine. It is more important for the founder and leaders to know what roles they need and to feel they have the right people to address those needs than it is for the organization to look good on an org chart.

This is a good time to get familiar with these five major areas of marketing and where they can help you create value for your idea, your product, your organization.

- Corporate marketing
- Demand generation
- Marketing operations
- Product marketing
- Field marketing

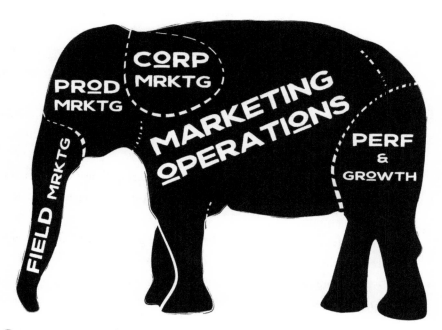

Corporate Marketing

This is the core of your company's communication to your internal teams as well as your external audiences. We talked to more than a few founders who think of corporate marketing as *marketing but without revenue*. No lead gen, no customer events. We can understand the desire to think of this role in that way. More important, however, is to think of what this role *does* do.

The corporate marketing function is responsible for core messaging, positioning, and brand *of your company*, not specific products. It is the central terminal, the hub, that everyone goes through. It is the collection point for what goes out from your organization, and it can be a central location for what comes into your organization. It is your marketing Grand Central Station.

The following responsibilities typically fall into this role, though they may not all be separate teams or even separate people:

- **Brand:** Brand's goal is to create a lasting impression among customers and, as a result, improve sales and market share. They define the voice and visual design of the brand and ensure a consistent and effective brand message and experience.

- **Public relations (press, media, and communications):** PR helps you build and manage your reputation, generally by working with the media. They'll help you get your story out, often by persuading journalists to write about you, but also via social media, helping you get speaking engagements, and other tactics.

- **Social:** Social involves managing your brand and communications on social media. It may include running marketing campaigns on social channels as well.

- **Content:** Content marketing involves creating blog posts, articles, ebooks, infographics, or any other content used to engage prospects and customers.

- **Influencer and analyst relations:** These groups build and manage relationships with analysts, industry experts, bloggers, and others who influence purchasing decisions in your industry.

- **Digital, web, and design:** They design and create your website, ads, and other visuals for your marketing programs.

These roles, people, and teams all work together to create your company's brand experience. We have both had experiences where a well-run corporate marketing organization was able to gain and share feedback with operations and finance, and even product and sales, based on what they were seeing and hearing in the field. They are the group that gets the prospect to say, "Oh, I've heard of you," on that first phone call.

In the early days of your startup, you won't have a separate corporate marketing group. But by the time you have multiple products, you'll be ready to have a corporate marketing group.

Corporate marketing = Grand Central Station

Demand Generation (aka Performance or Growth Marketing)

If there ever was a place for leads, leads, and more leads, this is the place! This is what most founders think of as *marketing*. How do I get more leads? What does my pipeline look like, and how do I accelerate it? Gimme leads.

What most demand generation marketers will tell you is that the better question and better goal is, how do I make the connection between my buyer and the opportunity to buy? Just like corporate marketing is your Grand Central Station, this role is your revenue hub. And while they can offer insights on your product organization, this role is likely more closely aligned with sales and your website to bring in potential buyers.

Andy Johns, VP of growth for Wealthfront, says it best: "Finance owns the flow of cash in and out of a company. Growth owns the flow of customers in and out of a product."[3]

This role is not some engine that just cranks out offers. Good demand generation marketers focus on marketing for customer acquisition and customer retention. This role is increasingly focused on the full value of the customer relationship throughout the life cycle.

They think across four goals and objectives:

Customer lifetime value (CLTV) ⇧

Customers ⇧

Time (to purchase) ⇩

Cost ⇩

How do I get as many customers as possible interested in our products, as quickly as possible, while trying to reduce costs over time? And how do I think about the lifetime value of the customer beyond just the initial transaction? How do they talk about us during their lifetime? Are they an advocate or a detractor? Do they bring in other customers or repel them?

Lauren Vaccarello of Box says:

> Measuring overall success on the lead is the wrong metric. I can generate 10,000 leads for you by standing on a corner and saying, "Hey everyone! Whoever signs up for this program gets a free iPad," and if I do that in front of AT&T Park during a Giants game, I can get your 10,000 leads. But those leads aren't going to matter.

---

3   "Indispensable Growth Frameworks from My Years at Facebook, Twitter, and Wealthfront," First Round Review, http://firstround.com/review/indispensable-growth-frameworks-from-my-years-at-facebook-twitter-and-wealthfront.

Demand generation marketers are frequently your biggest risk takers and your most analytical marketers, which is what we love about them. They want the comfort of data and insights but are willing to take risks. Those risks are in constantly experimenting with the way they generate interest in your customers and draw them to the product. The ad or the offer they put out in the market is frequently just one of several that they have created to test which one is best. As discussed in later chapters, even when an ad or offer performs really well, there is still constant testing to evolve the connections you make with your valuable customers and improve.

Demand generation = Mad scientists and alchemists

Marketing Operations

Marketing operations is the often overlooked red-headed stepchild of marketing. But the operations organization makes your business hum and can reduce costs while making the rest of marketing shine. Just like a COO (chief operating officer) helps run your entire business, your marketing operations person keeps your marketing organization running. For many businesses, this role can be a bit of a catchall for marketing, and an overwhelming amount of responsibility can be placed on this role.

They have three main responsibilities: technology, processes, and training.

Marketing operations is in charge of your MarTech stack (your marketing technology solutions). Marketing operations will be part of determining new solutions; it will own purchasing of technology and help install and manage it. They are not merely doers but take a strategic view of making the best selections at the best time for the best value. They make sure that the data in those systems is correct and accurate and that the organization gets the correct insights or analysis on that information in a timely manner.

There are currently over 6,800 MarTech solutions available to the marketing organization.[4] Many of them sound very promising and—at the right time and for the right goal—might well be the right solution for your organization. Just 10 years ago, there were only a few hundred solutions, and every year the number of new companies in the space skyrockets. Having a great operations person who can stay abreast of the wealth of solutions and know what to use and when is—in itself—a full-time job.

This role is central to your processes and how you start structuring your people to manage those processes. A simple example is how to qualify a lead or how to use your technology to make sure that lead gets to the right person at the right time. Based on your business goals, they make sure you have the right processes and systems in place to meet them. If, for instance, you have a business goal to drive revenue for a month and you want to use an offer for 15% off, if you don't have the right technology to accurately reflect that in the sale, you don't

---

4   Scott Brinker, "Marketing Technology Landscape Supergraphic (2018): Martech 5000 (Actually 6,829)," ChiefMarTec.com, April 24, 2018, https://chiefmartec.com/2018/04/marketing-technology-landscape-supergraphic-2018.

have your people trained on how to use your technology, or if that offer isn't correctly used in the purchasing process, your goals will fail.

As new technologies or products or processes come into your organization, your valuable talent will need to get up to speed and trained on those solutions quickly. Even the most simplistic-looking technology can upend your processes. Your operations person needs to be constantly looking at all the levers to help you be successful. Erica Brescia says, "A lot of founders wait too long to hire someone to help on the operations side."

The operations person is typically one of the later hires that a founder will make. This is a mistake. Having a strong person who can run the organization and keep it moving will pay off in dividends as you grow the organization and your business. They are often seen as an expenditure for the company. However, a good operations person will lower marketing costs. By thinking of your profits as revenue minus costs, a good operations person directly helps with profits by managing those costs and making the process of generating revenue more efficient and effective.

Marketing operations = Teacher, accountant, traffic cop

Product Marketing

Lea Hickman, partner at Silicon Valley Product Group, says:

> Product marketing can play a make-it-or-break-it role within the organization…If your sales force doesn't understand how to acquire new customers, or your customer success organization doesn't understand how to retain those customers and potential-ly even upsell them, that creates a gap where a competitor can come in and basically take business away.

Product marketing is the most misunderstood marketing function. Is it product, or is it marketing? This gets more muddled because in startups, often the product manager is the product marketer, and even in larger organizations, product marketing may be part of the product organization. There is definitely overlap, and we highly recommend that however you organize, product marketing should be part of or at least "joined at the hip" with product.

So what is product marketing?

Greg Powell, head of brand and product marketing at Fundbox, says that product marketing is about "bringing the market to the product and the product to the market."

Product marketing sits at the intersection of product management, sales, and marketing and at its core is about understanding customers. The job of the product marketer is to get the products in front of the customer, wherever they are, and to help them understand how the products can help them. That includes ensuring that sales understands how to talk about and sell the product and that customers understand how to use it. If you like the traditional funnel analogy for marketing, you can think about it as the lower part of the funnel. Product marketing focuses on engaging, converting, and retaining customers.

What does it mean tactically? Product managers write messaging and positioning for products and features, run product launches, understand and segment users, gather product requirements, determine pricing, create sales enablement tools to help sales close deals, create customer case studies and product collateral, do competitive analysis, and collect market insights.

In startups, product managers often do these things, or they are split between product and marketing, if they happen. Earlier, we talked about corporate marketing as being responsible for messaging and positioning as well. The difference here is that product marketers are product focused, while corporate marketers are company and brand focused. In a small startup, you may have one person or small group that covers all of marketing. In the very early days, when your product *is* your company, a well-rounded product marketer who can be a utility player is often a good choice for that first hire, particularly for B2B businesses. But as you grow, you may want to separate these out.

Powell recommends:

> After the product launches, product managers may tend to focus on the existing customer population. Where product marketing can really help complement that product management skill set is to look outside the company's walls and figure out who you're not talking to, your prospects, and figure out what they think. Because that might be a much, much different story.

Product marketing = Quarterback

Field Marketing

Your brand may be the face you portray to the world, but the field marketing team is the face that your audiences get to experience directly. Often thought of as event marketing, field marketing is the local presence—in the field—of your organization. They connect locally to your customers and prospects and audiences and make that direct connection with them. You aren't likely to need a field marketing team or even a field marketer unless your path to reach your customers is conferences or other live events. But if and when you start organizing your own big customer events or even having a presence at other big conferences, you'll understand why this role exists.

What often happens with field marketing is that the organization sends their least knowledgeable people for "floor duty" at a show or event, and their job is to get leads or scan badges for information. This usually results in a big list of irrelevant contacts that becomes a distraction more than anything else and doesn't take advantage of the value that field marketing can create.

Field marketing is a direct connection with your customer and should be closely aligned with your sales organization. Because it is directly connected with the customer, you should have knowledgeable people in those roles who know the product and service you are presenting, or they should be adequately trained and prepared to have those conversations. While this has typically been a one-way conversation consisting of the organization talking at the customer in exchange for their information, it is increasingly a two-way dialogue consisting of getting information, feedback, and insight from that customer into the product team and the rest of the organization.

Your field marketing team may know what works (or not) faster than any other part of the marketing organization. If you are trying a new message and you see the glazed-over look in your audience's eyes, you know it is not working—probably faster than you will through a message on the website. The key point of field marketing is to empower the teams to think this way: "We provide valuable feedback and partner with sales to help connect with customers." Most field marketing organizations are thought of as the team that assembles the booth or books rooms for the conference attendees. They are—or can be—much more than that.

David Rich, a long-time experiential marketer, says, "What we're really trying to do is engage with the consumer community so deeply that they begin to take on the task of evangelizing the brand themselves."

Field marketing = Winning hearts and minds

Putting It All Together

You don't need these roles all at once, and not every role needs a distinct person in it at the beginning. Some of your talented marketing staff may have two or three of these roles for a while. Over time you can think about building out and scaling your organization appropriately as it makes sense. You may never need a field marketing *organization*, but knowing how it can help you grow your business is important. From a team of one to a team of 50 or 500, these roles all fit together to help the business connect to the customer and make internal connections with sales and product. Which ones you need and how much will be determined by your market and the best ways to reach them.

As you start out, often it is more about fit than it is about structure. If there is great chemistry between your performance person and your sales leader, leverage that connection. As we discuss in later chapters, you should think about this as levers to pull to help you achieve your goal or outcome at each stage. What are you trying to accomplish, and how do these roles best fit to help accelerate or optimize your goals? Each of the following chapters discusses your goals and objectives at a certain stage to help you fit these roles into those.

As a founder, you have to be the whole elephant until you can bring on others to take on the other elephantine features. You are the ears until you find someone to be them for you, so to speak.

Let's take this definition of marketing—as the connection between the customer and your sales and product organizations—forward into the first stage of your startup's growth.

3
PROVE THE IDEA

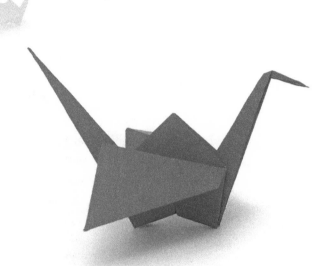

The looming question at this stage:

- I have this great idea; where do I start?

This chapter will cover:

- Defining, validating, and sizing the market
- Developing your pitch

I read about a company called Rosen Hotel. From day one they wanted to provide health benefits to their employees. But it was really expensive because their employees were housekeepers and waitstaff and yard maintenance folks. A lot of them were first-generation immigrants [and] came over with a lot of health issues. There wasn't a high wage base.

Rosen did some creative things with their health benefits to improve employees' health, improve employee retention, increase the net promoter scores on their hotels, and cut their health care expenses by so much that they were able to add a new benefit, which was free college tuition for their employees and their employees' kids!

I read the case study and I was like, *That's what I want to do. I want to bring that to every other employer in America.*

So begins Cheryl Kellond's story about founding Apostrophe Healthcare, to "build the health plan that can fix America."

As an entrepreneur, you begin with a big idea, a problem only you can solve. Maybe it's a new solution to a long-standing problem, or maybe you're solving a problem people didn't even realize they had. Maybe you knew you were destined to be an entrepreneur, or you may have tried to talk yourself out of this crazy idea, but the more you talk to people about it and evolve your idea, one thing is for sure: you *have* to do this.

The reality is that most startups don't survive long enough to deliver any returns for their investors. It turns out that having the idea is actually the easy part. Very few companies successfully turn that idea into a viable product and a successful business.

Focus of This Stage

You know that starting a company will take over your life, so not only does the problem you choose to focus on need to be worth solving, but you need to be excited to focus on it indefinitely, and the opportunity needs to be big enough to turn into a successful business. As a founder, you can increase your chances of success by doing extra work upfront to *prove the idea*. This stage is about that process.

Proving the idea is confirming that there is a need in the market and figuring out who has that need and what exactly they need. This is a crucial step that can set a startup off on the right (or wrong) path. This is where marketing first makes an appearance and adds significant value in the life of a startup.

The Role of Marketing

At this stage, the role of marketing is pretty straightforward: it is about figuring out who your market is and what they want.

Dale Sakai, a successful CEO and strategic planning expert who has run multiple companies, including Incyte Group, which helped companies increase valuations by optimizing strategic plans, says:

> Fundamentally marketing is about understanding the marketplace, what the market wants, and what your target segment really wants and building an offering to meet that market...That's pretty common sense.
>
> Build a product that people want. Don't build a product and then figure out if somebody wants it, because usually that doesn't work well...
>
> Products fail mainly because they don't deliver value to the market. In other words, the person who conceived of the product or the offering really didn't ask the questions of the market: What do you want? What is required? What is the need? What feature or functionality you want? So the entrepreneur or the product manager used their opinion to determine what to bring to the market, and their thinking wasn't reflective of the market.

Many entrepreneurs start developing products before truly answering these fundamental questions and the question that precedes all of them: *Who is your market?*

Outside investors will want these answers before they invest. More data and information will, of course, make your case stronger. Steve Mankoff, general partner at TDF Ventures, explains:

A lot of times entrepreneurs have a great idea, and they'll go pursue that idea. Some will, based on a single customer or their own idea, go build it and then try to find some customers or some potential fit.

Other entrepreneurs will go out and leverage their network and talk to 50, 100, or more potential customers. They get a lot of different market data points and have a much deeper customer perspective of the market from the start. I find that the second group tends to get better traction and better results.

So you can't expect to just go survey customers and have them tell you what to build. It's about going and spending a lot of time with potential customers and going deep in the market to really understand what the critical requirements are, what the differentiators are, and how your idea marries up with the market to be successful.

What about stealth startups? Figuring out who your market is is important for all startups, even for those startups trying to be in stealth mode. The only way to know if you truly have a business is to connect with your market. In fact, Maha Ibrahim, general partner at Canaan Partners, advises, "I'm just not a fan of that stealth concept because, as an early-stage company, you need as much feedback from the marketplace as possible. And you can only do that when you're talking to customers and talking to partners who have lived in it for a while."

Defining Your Market

There is often a tension at this stage in defining the market to go after. Investors want to fund big opportunities with big markets. As a result, there is pressure to define your market broadly. This can often be rationalized to capture as many customers as possible and not leave anything on the table. Founders may fear that if they go too narrow, their product and brand will be associated with that narrow market—that they will appear to be a niche solution. While this may seem counterintuitive, a narrow targeted approach may be the best course. By going too broad too early you risk not satisfying the needs of the different segments, creating a negative impression when you can't address their needs, or spreading your product development too thin to address those various needs. When you try to make everyone happy, you make no one happy.

You can do both at once. You can paint a picture for your potential investors of the large market you plan to serve (your TAM, or total addressable market) while starting with a narrow focus, targeting just one segment (your SAM, or serviceable addressable market) whose needs you can meet successfully now. Focusing on a single thing will enable you to do it really well. If you can gain traction and make a set of customers happy and loyal, it will help your investor story. Later in the chapter we cover assessing your market size (TAM analysis) in more depth.

Yes, you can build a business on one or two market segments and later expand. Amazon is a great example of this. Jeff Bezos claims he always wanted to build an "everything store." Early on, he focused solely on selling books to book buyers who were on the internet. He used his success there to create a beachhead. He was able to focus on building and expanding a platform and sales channel so that now Amazon serves a broad market that is buying nearly anything and everything online. Though Amazon was known in its early years as a place to buy books online, they managed to expand the position they hold in consumers' minds.

This idea of focus isn't just played out at the world's largest companies; it is seen in organizations that are just getting started. Ian Roncoroni was tired of getting his name mangled—misspelled, mispronounced—every single time he interacted with a business over the phone. So he decided to do something about it. His company, NextCaller, helps businesses authenticate the caller and then add additional data from social platforms so call centers and service companies know exactly who they are talking with and can create a better personal experience.

But, as is common with organizations just starting out, new customers started pushing them into new directions. Soon, NextCaller was developing products and marketing for five different buying centers in the organization. What started as a simple purpose quickly morphed and expanded. Costs inflated as they struggled to support five product lines with five distinct purposes for all these customers. Revenues slowed as their margins shrank. In short, they were spread too thin to manage their now complex business.

Roncoroni spent a great deal of time with customers and potential customers listening to what their needs were. With advice from investors and a strong network of mentors, Ian made the counterintuitive decision to focus on one product offering. It turns out that institutions were concerned with the security of their interactions—of knowing that Ian was actually Ian—and if that was solved they could focus their efforts on a great customer experience and quickly start addressing their customer's concerns.

Their focus paid off as the company is now on a hyper-growth trajectory, with extra fuel from a new round of funding. Scaling back and focusing actually put them on a path for exponential growth as well as a better use of money and resources into one product instead of being spread across several.

Upfront work focusing on a specific market and understanding the desires, needs, and behaviors of that market deeply can help you down the road. As Dale Sakai explains:

> Pick a target that has a propensity to want to buy your solution, where you know what their requirements are and what their needs are and what functionality or features they're looking for. If you can build for them and you know who they are, you can also create a marketing campaign to actually reach those folks, and if you've got it right, logically they will probably buy it because you know you're meeting their requirements.

At this stage, you are looking for credible evidence to validate that there are enough people willing to spend enough on your solution for you to build a real business. Although you have a vision for a much larger market, focusing on a specific market with problems you can solve today will enable you to go deep enough to truly understand your customers, their needs, and how they buy to build out your product and go-to-market approach. Gaining clarity about who these customers are and what they care about will help you answer important product and marketing questions as you go forward.

Understanding the Market

Kate Bradley Chernis, founder and CEO of Lately, spent years consulting to marketing departments at companies of all sizes. They all struggled to keep their marketing campaigns organized and consistent. Kate had built a series of complex spreadsheets that became a lifeline for her customers. When a friend convinced her to convert those spreadsheets into a software solution, she already knew her customers and their pain intimately and had pre-validated the idea with what was effectively an early paper prototype of the product. Her team was able to mock up a software solution based on her spreadsheets to further test and validate it with the market.

Like Kate, founders often have some domain expertise. But just because you have some expertise in an area doesn't mean you don't have blind spots. This is particularly true for startups that are aiming at whitespace, doing something that hasn't been done before.

Making an early investment in market research is a great way to gain deeper understanding of the market and set your organization on the right path from the start. Market research is simply the act of gathering information about consumers' needs and preferences. The data and customer stories from market research can provide a guiding light for your company and instill confidence from early investors.

There are multiple ways of approaching this early market research that don't need to be very costly. In all cases, collecting a combination of quantitative and qualitative data is the ideal scenario. The numbers will help you understand the breadth of applicability, and they'll keep you from falling into the trap of believing that outlying voices are representative when they are not. The anecdotes will provide color to help you understand the data.

Quantitative research generally consists of industry reports and surveys. Online surveys are generally the easiest option if you can reach your market that way. Several online survey solutions will allow you to create and run surveys targeted to defined audiences for little money. You can also run surveys at trade shows or other physical locations where you know you'll find the right audience.

To fill out your picture and understand the data with qualitative studies, you can run in-person interviews with potential buyers, users, influencers, and any other relevant experts. Use those interviews to fill out a more complete picture of your market. Where do these people work and live? What are their greatest challenges? What do they care most about? What would help them do their jobs better? After several of these interviews, you'll begin to see patterns and probably some conflicting data. This will help deepen your knowledge and should provide ideas that you can further validate with quantitative surveys to draw conclusions.

Erik Larson is the founder and CEO of Cloverpop, a cloud-based software startup that helps businesses track, communicate, and improve decisions. He started out looking to build a product that could help people achieve their goals. The very early days of his company were spent running countless research studies to understand human behavior with respect to goal setting and testing various ideas. He read a lot of research on the subject and ran his own studies online and in person. He created many prototypes to test whether he could impact success. Erik believed if he could help people achieve their goals and be successful, then he could figure out how to turn it into a business.

Through these studies, Erik gained a wealth of understanding about goal setting, success, and decision-making. Eventually a couple of key ahas led to the formation of the business: he realized that the people who were deciding to achieve a goal achieved success at much greater rates, and that it is possible to correct for biases and help people make dramatically better decisions.

These were his first proof points that he had a business opportunity.

You can find subjects for these interviews from your surveys, by advertising online, or by going wherever your target segment hangs out with a pile of gift cards. We've run surveys on iPads at trade shows and via websites, giving away anything from Amazon and Starbucks gift cards to analyst research to free flights.

Whether in person or online, there is an art to writing a good unbiased survey or conducting an interview. How you ask questions matters, as does the number of survey takers. If you have the ability, you may want to hire someone with experience to help. Otherwise, there are books and online resources that can provide more detailed guidance. In all cases the approach is to develop hypotheses about your market and test it, just like you did in high school science class. Define your objectives and hypothesis. Determine a plan to reach the target group. Create questions to validate—or invalidate—your hypothesis. Collect the data. Analyze it. Try to disprove your idea.

Five Tips for Conducting Market Research
1. **Know your objectives:** Be clear about the questions you are trying to answer.
2. **Survey the right people and enough of them:** Make sure you are reaching your actual target customers and ensure your survey population is large enough to be reliable.
3. **Don't forget the extra questions:** Include demographic questions so you can segment your responses. You may find surprises when you look at the data different ways.
4. **Don't lead the witness:** Review your questions to make sure they are objective and don't compel respondents to answer a certain way.
5. **Don't ignore the results:** The results may contradict your beliefs and desires. Pay attention. Corroborate with a follow up if you need to. But don't ignore them.

The goal of these surveys is to test and validate your hypotheses about your prospective customers, their needs, your solution, and your business. This is a good point to start tracking hypotheses and learnings for all the key aspects of your business. If you're following a Lean startup model, you may want to use Steve Blank's Customer Development Worksheets, Alexander Osterwalder's Business Model Canvas, Ash Maurya's Lean Canvas, or similar tools. Whatever approach you use, as you home in on your product concept, you should be similarly focusing in on the key aspects of your business that will be essential to your success. This may include:
- The problem you are solving
- Your solution
- Your target customers

- Your unique value proposition for those customers
- Your competitive differentiation
- The channels you can use to reach your customers
- Critical partners
- Your revenue model
- Your cost structure
- Whatever you believe is the most important metric to track for your business

The interviews and surveys can provide great insights to help determine these other aspects of your business, including your go-to-market strategy, positioning, and messaging as you begin to sell to your customers.

iPads and other tablets are now commonplace. People can be seen reading, web surfing, playing games, and even writing, coding, and drawing on them. But when the first iPads came out in 2010, there were many questions from the market about what they'd be used for.

Jill worked in Adobe's Creative Suite business at the time. Her group saw an opportunity for designers to use these devices in their workflow as an additional tool or even a replacement for the journals that they carried everywhere and sketched in. Sketching on tablets was a wildly unpopular idea among professional designers at the time. Steve Jobs was also skeptical and refused to make a stylus for drawing on the iPad.

Jill's team conducted many interviews with designers to understand the opportunity. They asked many open-ended questions to understand why they carried those sketchbooks, how they chose them, what they liked and disliked about them, how they used them, and what they did with their sketches. They found that designers often sketched concepts in their sketchbooks that they wanted to use in their work. But they had to go through multiple steps to copy or recreate that work when they got to the office. This was their opening—a pain point that they could address for their customers. The seed project they began based on that idea and the learnings from those interviews became a core part of Adobe Creative Cloud, fueling Adobe's transition to the cloud and new growth.

You may need to get creative in trying to reach your customers. In Cheryl Kellond's case, in the early days of Apostrophe, originally named Airstream Health, she rented an Airstream and drove it through rural Colorado, providing quick chronic care and diabetes screenings in school district parking lots to meet and learn from potential customers. This trip led to much deeper understanding of their customers and learnings that drove important decisions for their business.

> We initially had a lot of back-and-forth discussion about what we wanted to do about a provider network.
>
> So we were up in Fort Morgan Colorado for about 45 minutes, and we had the first few people that had scheduled appointments with us come in, and we heard the same story from all of them. No, they hadn't gotten their free wellness checkup because they would always get this $300 bill after they went in. So it wasn't really free. None of them had gotten their diabetes screening or their fibroid screening in a really long period of time...
>
> So during the lunch break I walked two blocks down the street to the local hospital where they're getting this done, and I walk into the lab, and I was like, "Hey, what's going on?" And the woman goes, "Oh yeah, those are our insurance rates. These people should just come in and ask for our cash-based pricing." She handed me this price list. Those $300 worth of lab tests on a cash pay basis, 40 bucks!
>
> They didn't know.
>
> It was the moment for us that we said, hey you know what? Forget your direct contracting, tracking, networking, and all the ways we can build this network out. We just need to be able to take advantage of the cash pay pricing that already exists in the market. How do we set up a health plan that's really natively designed to do that? Because these amazing rates and these stair rates are already out there, and these people on high-deductible

health plans are paying all their healthcare costs out of their pocket anyways and they're getting charged these enormous insurance rates. So it was a pretty formative moment for us.

Whatever the approach, you'll walk away from this phase with a strong hypothesis and some data to support:

- Your target market
- The customer's unmet or underserved needs
- Your value proposition

Use this information to begin defining your minimum viable product to support that value proposition and meet those needs for that customer.

You may very well need to run several rounds of interviews and surveys and test many prototypes before you get clarity and confidence about your target market. The old notion our grandmothers gave us is critically important: an ounce of prevention is worth a pound of cure. Doing even a little bit of work at this stage will save you enormous unseen headaches at later stages.

Bruce Cleveland, founding partner at Wildcat Ventures, warns: "Keep your expenses as low as you possibly can. Get a statistically relevant sampling of the market that you believe you want to go after with people you don't know before you ever lay a single line of code, and before you ever spend a dollar on rent or on salaries." The desire at this stage is strong to go, move, drive, build. Market research may not feel tangible or feel like action, but it is about making sure that when you do go fast, you aim in the right direction.

Assessing Your Market

You'll likely need to create a TAM analysis for your pitch and validate your assessment of the opportunity for your business. The common approach to creating a TAM is to do a top-down analysis, leveraging industry research from Gartner, IDC, Hoovers, or other companies with relevant reports. This is the simplest approach to reach an overall market size number, but it doesn't take into account the complexities of your business and the market.

A better approach is to combine the top-down analysis with a bottom-up analysis, making it more real. The bottom-up analysis looks at any data you have from your early sales efforts and can collect on your competition and substitutes. You then multiply the current price by the number of units you estimate you can sell. This approach requires some assumptions about the type and number of customers you can serve and how quickly, as well as how much they'll buy at what price.

You can add additional layers to this analysis by looking at how much additional value you can add over your competition and the additional sales that you'll be able to capture as a result. When including the TAM in your pitch, Mei Chuong, COO and co-founder of Zeuss, recommends: "If you can focus on the bottom-up and the value theory, you can make a really good case, and VCs find it very impressive for the company at an early stage to get an estimated number based on those two approaches." She suggests, "You should focus not just on the TAM but on the SAM, or serviceable addressable market. This is the segment of the TAM that our current product that we have in place can service today. So when we say focus, we are saying: Where are we selling? What can we sell, and how can we sell now? How can we acquire customers quickly?"

Pulling It Together: The Pitch

Kevin Eyers says:

> When I invest in an early-stage company, I need to have a solid belief in the founder. Not just as somebody who's going to run the business, but as a person. What's your journey? What have you learned through this? What have you learned from the successes and failures? How do you embrace discomfort? I want to understand them and understand if they're aware of themselves, as well. Because one thing that I've found from investing in companies is that have gone well, and some have gone to zero. And the common element is the founder. My mistakes were when I did not trust my gut and listened to people tell me how successful the business model was or how the company was destined for success, but I didn't see it in the founder. So that's really one of the things I look for.

We're assuming that if you're reading this chapter and going through this phase, there's a reasonable chance you'll be looking for some early funding. Even if you are bootstrapping your company, getting your story down and having a pitch for early stakeholders will prove useful.

Once you have the data and customer understanding to convince you of the opportunity, you can build that into a business case and craft the story. This will likely be in the form of a pitch deck and presentation.

The most important part of your pitch is the story, and the story you tell investors is not exactly the same as the one you tell customers. What lights up investors is not the same thing that lights up customers. Customers want to know how you'll make their lives better today. Investors want to know how you're going to create a huge successful business.

Steve Mankoff echoes Kevin's sentiment and adds:

> When I'm looking at investment, I'm investing in people. It's people first, great ideas second, and third is the potential market for that idea and understanding that. Too many founders come in and they just kind of want to walk through their slide deck without telling me the story of the startup. Why did you do it? Everything has a story behind it. And I think stories really help convey passion message and belief.

Maha Ibrahim considers a different priority order when judging investments:

> As a general rule, I'm looking for markets. So above all, I need to be investing in a company that can house a multiple-billion-dol-lar outcome. So size of market and timing is table stakes, and if I can't see my way to there being a massive outcome for the company, I will not invest in it. A part of that is timing: is the timing right for this technology, for this opportunity to really al-low this company to excel and grow? Then I look at team: is this team nimble enough, are they intelligent enough, are they driven enough to navigate the perils of startup and opportunities of a

startup in this opportunity, in this time frame, in this agency of life? So I'm mainly looking at those two criteria, and then, in the context of enterprise and consumer, I think about what profile of company and team will allow that company to grow.

Like Steve Mankoff, Maha Ibrahim expects the CEO to be the number one evangelist:

The CEO and team need to be a chief sales officer and a chief visionary of the company. Yes, they need to execute; yes, they need to be able to hire...but first and foremost, they need to set the tone for the entire company and investors and customers of where the company is going, what they aspire to do. So in that first meeting, I'm really looking for a CEO to make me a believer. When I invest, it is usually because that CEO is able to convince me that there's a massive opportunity for what they do and that they're uniquely positioned to take advantage of that.

The Story

Crafting a pitch is like writing any other good story. Stories bring in people and engage them. Investors hear tons of pitches and see as many slide decks. If you want to stand out, paint a picture with a compelling narrative. Who is your protagonist? What does the world look like at the start of the story? Why does it matter? What is your vision of the future? How is it different and better?

Founding the company may have started with you—your personal experience or problem or one that you discovered. But now is the time to flip that story on its head and communicate how and why it should be important to your audience. Whose life are you going to change, and how are they representative of a larger group? Why does it matter? Why are you best suited to solve this problem? The market research you just completed will be invaluable in developing this story.

Even if you plan to bootstrap your company, to hire, to develop partnerships, to bring in early customers, and to build confidence in the business opportunity, you'll need to craft the story and help each one of these audiences see how they fit into it.

A good story is just that: a story. That doesn't mean that it should be made up. It should be authentic, but it also needs to be compelling. Investors are looking for a reason *not* to invest. If you can't clearly articulate your vision in a compelling way and explain what is driving you, you'll have a hard time getting funding.

We know the origin stories of most great brands, and the garage or dorm rooms where they had their modest beginnings. This book has an origin story, too. The two of us were chatting at a dinner about the similarities of our experiences working with early-stage companies. We began to write a blog post on practical advice for founders. That post just kept getting longer and longer and longer.

An important piece of the story is how your solution is an innovation. How is it different and going to change the world as we know it in a way that matters?

Four Tips for Crafting Your Story from Nancy Duarte

1. Make the customer the hero. In a typical story, the hero is stuck until someone comes along and helps them, mentors them, gives them tools to move forward. Your job is to give them those tools—your product—to help them be the hero.
2. Great storytelling isn't just marketing. Great leader stories—your origin story—help get people excited to work with or for you, to wake up energized to help you, from the second their feet hit the floor in the morning till their head hits their pillow at night.
3. A great story is emotional fuel people need to stick with you. As employees or customers, the story fuels belief in what you can accomplish together.
4. As a leader, your story offers credibility to investors to tell them who you are and what you stand for.

Defining the Category

An important part of crafting your story is defining the category in which your product or service exists. Are you entering an existing category with an improvement on an existing solution, or is your product creating a whole new category? This distinction will become important because the two scenarios require very different go-to-market approaches. For example, when Jill ran marketing at Freshworks, she was selling customer support software and CRM. In an already crowded marketplace with well-known competitors like Salesforce and Zendesk, potential buyers were looking for solutions but often started at competitor's sites due to their strong brand awareness. Her team's challenge was to capture some of that market's attention and convince them that the Freshworks products were different and better. In Jill's role at Cloverpop, she and her colleagues are selling a brand-new type of software that helps businesses track, communicate, and improve decision-making. They need to identify and reach people who might have an interest and educate them that a solution even exists, before starting to sell.

Analysis of US venture capital–backed tech startups founded from 2000 to 2015 by Al Ramadan and his coauthors found that category kings earned 76% of the market capitalization of their entire market categories.[5] Bruce Cleveland explains the importance of defining your category:

> The first role of marketing (and this is usually the CEO and the team) is to figure out what category you're in. Category is another name for a problem. What problem are you solving? What's the name of that problem?
>
> You might think this is relatively simply to put a few words on paper, but think about what [Marc] Benioff did with the sign "no software." Now, was Salesforce really no software?...In one simple sign, without putting a bunch of technical gobbledygook out there around multitenancy and all these technical bits, he conveyed to potential customers that installing, implementing, and bringing up enterprise software is really hard, it's really expensive, and you shouldn't have to do it. In that one sign, he conveyed a new category. He actually chose to go after an existing category of applications, CRM, with his first product offerings. But what he

---

5   Al Ramadan, Dave Peterson, Christopher Lockhead, and Kevin Maney, *Play Bigger: How Pirates, Dreamers, and Innovators Create and Dominate Markets* (New York: Harper Business: 2016).

really was conveying was a new category of software.

If we think about Steve Jobs, Steve didn't create PCs; he certainly didn't create the first phone, the first watch, or the first tablet. What he did was redefine or reimagine what those categories could be and was very clever about explaining what they did to consumers.

The question is whether the category is big enough that this company is even worth doing. If it is, how do you become a category king? Trying to enter someone else's kingdom is fraught with peril. It's very challenging to challenge a category king.

Many companies have smashed themselves against the rocks of category creation. Many cheat their way into it by trying to change some small part of the category to claim victory. In the CRM space alone, companies tried win eCRM, or CCRM (collaborative). Just placing another letter in the space won't do it. Creating a category is heady work and more than just dipping your toe in new category waters. It requires understanding the needs in the market and aligning your solution to capture those needs. It doesn't end there; it then means educating the market, creating that space in people's minds, and making sure that your buyer and the marketplace in general think of you as the leader in that space. This is more than just you planting a flag and claiming victory. The point is that categories don't just happen overnight and should not be attempted without strategic purpose and planning.

Creating the Pitch Deck

Perspectives vary on the number of slides to include in a pitch deck, but you should generally plan to present in about 20 minutes and include the following info:

- **Basics:** Include your company name, logo, tagline, and contact information. This slide should quickly and clearly communicate who you are and what your startup does.
- **Vision:** How do you see the world, and why did you launch this startup?

- **Problem:** What is the problem you are solving? How great is the problem? Why is it important to solve? You've answered this question with all that early market research.
- **Solution:** What is your insight? How are you solving the problem? Is it a new technology, a platform, a new business model?
- **Product demo:** Show what your product does and how it works so investors can visualize it.
- **Business model:** How are you going to generate revenue?
- **Market opportunity:** How big is the addressable market? How did you arrive at this number? Try to provide a bottom-up analysis here.
- **Competition and your differentiation:** Who are your competitors and what are their strengths? What are the substitute solutions? Why will your solution win?
- **Go-to-market approach:** How will you reach your market? How will you sell the product?
- **Traction:** Share any customer testimonials, press quotes, or early key metrics—anything that speaks to your success thus far. The metrics you're tracking are especially important, and investors often want to know that you are metrics driven. If you have compelling traction, this is likely to engage investors, so include it early.
- **Team:** Who is on your founding team, and why are you uniquely qualified to build this solution and take it to market? Include key advisors. At the seed stage, investors are betting on the team first, so you may want to cover this up front.
- **Ask:** How much are you raising? What are you asking for? What do you plan to do with the funding? What milestones do you plan to hit?

Four Pitching Tips from Kate Bradley Chernis

1. **Pitch the way you talk:** *"I learned in radio that something really important was to always talk like yourself. You would never read the weather and be like, 'There's cumulus clouds out and 62% chance of rain.' You'd be like, 'It's cloudy and grab an umbrella.'...You just sound weird when you're saying*

stuff that isn't something you would normally say. So I write my pitches out with all my slang words, however it is that I normally talk, then you certainly memorize it but you don't memorize, you end up learning it."

2. **Practice with mistakes:** *"I do this thing where I would put 20 pennies in a jar and have an empty jar next to me and I would do the pitch 20 times [moving a penny from one jar to the other each time]. I would do it through all the mistakes because you have to be able to come out of it, if you make a mistake live."*

3. **Practice on stage:** *"I go there beforehand, I do my pitch out loud, in the room. I don't care if people are setting up chairs. I like to stand there and get the feel of what the room is like so I'm not scared."*

4. **Be the loudest voice in the room:** *"When I go to a pitch event, I just yell. I don't care if I have a microphone, I always talk the loudest. It is important to project your voice and even make them jump a little bit because people are busy with their phones and all that."*

No matter which path you decide to take to tackle your chosen problem, it is of critical importance that you, the founder, are authentic. People can tell when you aren't being true. Do what works for you. Have your voice in the pitch and tell the story you want to tell. While the above list is a great guide, you know best what story you want to tell.

The Marketing Team at This Stage

At this stage, the founders are the marketing team. If you need specific help with doing market research, writing messaging to test, or creating your pitch deck, hire freelancers to help you. You should not need a marketing team yet.

Moving Forward

In this first phase, we focused on how you can make sure you are headed in a direction that will bring success by validating that you are building a product that people actually want, before writing any code or building a product. Have grand visions, but focus on a target group of people who will get lots of value from your product. And take the time to nail down your story, because it will be critical for bringing in investors, employees, customers, and partners. As Stewart Butterfield, founder of Slack and Flickr, said:

> If there was one piece of advice I wish I could phone back and give to myself, [it would be to] just concentrate on that story-telling part, on convincing people. Because if you can't do that, it doesn't matter how good the product is, it doesn't matter how good the idea was for the market, or what happens in the external factors.[6]

If you've done the market research to identify and validate your market, found some early potential customers who are demanding your offering, crafted your story (at least your first version), convinced yourself the idea has legs, and convinced investors to get on board, it is now time to go forward and start to build and prove the product.

---

6   "The Big Pivot: Stewart Butterfield, Co-founder and CEO of Slack," *Masters of Scale,* November 15, 2017, https://mastersofscale.com/stewart-butterfield-the-big-pivot.

4

PROVE THE PRODUCT

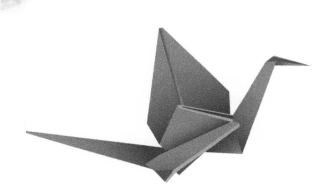

The looming question at this stage:
- What do we need to do to get to product/market fit?

This chapter will cover:
- Marketing's role in getting to product/market fit
- Investments to make at this stage
- Your first sales tools

Arjun Moorthy, founder and CEO of the B2C news rating startup OwlFactor, says:

> In our many pivots to find product/market fit I began to wonder
> if I'd even know what product/market fit would look like. I felt
> like we were discovering pieces of a giant puzzle in the dark and
> would run out of money before we saw the whole picture.

When we finally achieved product/market-fit, three signs made it obvious:

Users did not uninstall the product quickly.

Users reached out voluntarily to suggest features.

Users told their friends about our product, who also installed and used it.

The simplest indicator was the count of times a user said *love* in a user test when talking about our product...As we started to see people use the word *love* about our product, we started to feel that we had something of value.

Product/market fit, a term credited to venture capitalist Marc Andreessen, meaning "being in a good market with a product that can satisfy that market," is arguably the most critical milestone for any startup. He claimed that "the life of any startup can be divided into two parts: before product/market fit (call this BPMF) and after product/market fit (APMF). When you are BPMF, focus obsessively on getting to product/market fit. Do whatever is required to get to product/market fit."[7]

Focus of This Stage

This stage is all about getting to product/market fit.

A startup founder recently asked us, "What does marketing have to do with product/market fit?" If product/market fit is about proving there is a market with a need for your product and that you have the right core product for that market, you can think about marketing as the market part of the product/market fit equation.

---

7   Marc Andreessen, "The PMARCA Guide to Startups, Part 4: The Only Thing That Matters," originally published on his blog, blog.pmarca.com. That blog has since been taken down but is archived at https://pmarchive.com/guide_to_startups_part4.html.

Marketing is the market part of the product/market fit equation.

At this stage, many founders are focused on product, product, product. That is the critical first step, defining and building the product and validating it with the market. And it is an iterative and unpredictable process. Maha Ibrahim says:

> Those early days are incredibly critical in getting market feedback. It's all about what are the features that are causing my customers to use this product once and then come back and come back and come back without my having to pay to acquire that customer again. So those early days should be spent in very close communication and contact with the customer, whether it's enterprise or consumer, and really diving into what the features are, what the mechanics are of the product that are enticing the customers, that are attractive to customers, and what are aspects of the product that are less needed and what are aspects of the product that you don't have yet that really need to be put in place.

But there is more to proving product/market fit than building product. Steve Mankoff says, "Product is just one piece of the puzzle. That's clearly the first piece, but you need to be thinking early on about go-to-market and working on that and learning that and thinking how to scale it; that's where startups often hit the wall."

The role of marketing in this phase is heavily a product marketing one: helping the product team define and validate the right target customer, creating and testing early messaging and positioning, and starting to figure out how to reach that customer, which generally includes creating your first sales tools and content.

While writing this book, Jill was also working with startup Cloverpop on getting to product/market fit with their decision practices software. Never heard of decision practices software? You're not alone. Creating and validating a new category of product can be hard, even when it solves a real pain.

To get there, of course they focused on the product, trying to identify what made users come back repeatedly. They had many aha moments as they engaged with early customers. Some of them seem obvious in retrospect, but sometimes you have to live something to truly learn. For example, some of their initially enthusiastic early customers had trouble driving adoption of the tool in their organizations. Getting teams of people to change their existing process is hard. This is true, even if the new process is actually quicker and has proven value, if it seems longer and harder.

The resulting evolution from software that improves the process of decision-making to a system of record for decisions that makes it easy to record, track, communicate, and also improve decisions was transformational. Possibly even more impactful was the resulting clearer picture of their target customer and evolution of their product messaging and positioning. In addition, they were able to identify and develop high-value sales tools and onboarding programs that solved critical pieces of their product/market fit puzzle.

Beyond the Product

Marketing students generally learn about the Four Ps marketing mix:[8] product, price, promotion, and placement. This framework is basically about the importance of thinking holistically about your product. You need to put the right product in the right place, at the right price, at the right time for the right customer.

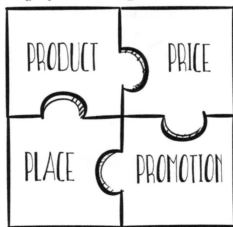

Four Ps marketing mix

---

8   The concept of the Four Ps marketing mix was coined by marketing professor E. Jerome McCarthy in the book *Basic Marketing: A Managerial Approach* (Homewood, IL: R. D. Irwin, 1960).

- **Product**, of course, refers to the features, benefits, and the unique value proposition of the good or service.
- **Price** is how much the customer pays and how they pay (e.g., platform fee plus subscription versus upfront). The price is linked to the customer's perceived value of the product. It is critical to understand their value and price sensitivity.
- **Promotion** is how you are telling your customer about your product. How do they find out and what additional marketing strategies are you using to entice them to consider and purchase? This category includes advertising, PR, special offers, and so on.
- **Placement** is how you reach your customer. Where can they get your product? Are you selling online or in box stores? Do the purchasers buy at trade shows? Do you have an inside sales team calling prospects?

All of these together are needed to define a compelling product offering.

It All Starts with the Customer

One common scenario for startups at this stage is this: You have a broadly applicable product but haven't figured out which verticals or departments truly need it. Your generic pitch is interesting and speaks to a common pain or desire. But you haven't hit the deep nerve that cuts across any one segment and makes them say, "I need this now. Where do I sign?"

Geoffrey Moore, in his book *Crossing the Chasm*, recommends that you focus on a single market, a beachhead, to win over a specific market and use it as a springboard to expand into neighboring markets.

The task for the entrepreneur at this stage is to define and test a hypothesis about which customers have the greatest need for your product or service, what features they value, and how to best sell to them. So the core of the work in this phase is:

- Anything that helps you better understand the needs and behaviors of your target segments.
- Developing messaging and content to test with these segments.
- Hustling to try to sell to these customers to see if it works.
- Learning and iterating to do it better.

If your startup focuses on a specific niche, this process may be easier because you know where to focus and can go deep to understand them and validate your offering.

Often entrepreneurs want to go after a large market to maximize opportunity and find themselves with a broadly applicable solution. That is great from the perspective of having a large total addressable market (TAM). However, to reach that market, you need to be able to focus and speak directly to buyers and users. That means you need to understand them and speak their language. But you can't focus on every segment at once. So, you need to figure out what segment feels the pain that you can solve most intensely and is willing to spend money on it. Start there.

To do this, as Steve Blank says, "get out of the building." Go where they are to understand the market and your potential customers.

Your Ideal Customer

Have you ever seen a movie or TV show where the actor pleads with the director to know "What is my motivation for this character?" Ideal customer profiles (ICPs) or personas are a way for organizations to understand their customers in that same way. Who are they and what do they want—what are they motivated by—to make the purchase? It is simply about thinking of your customers as a few simple examples to help you better connect with them.

Clearly defining your customer is one of the most important things you can do for your business. It provides focus and acts as a guide for everything you do. Once you know who you are building for, you can better home in on what features to prioritize, what channels to use to reach your customers, and what messaging to use in those channels. The ICP also helps your salespeople to know which prospects to focus their efforts on.

If you sell to businesses, your ICP should be at the company level and describe anything relevant, including industry, size, location, level of technological maturity, and so on.

For example, the ICP for a B2B SaaS help desk software company might be:

- Software as a Service (SaaS) businesses
- Small and mid-sized businesses

- Businesses with annual revenue greater than $20 million
- Businesses with a customer support team of 10–50 people
- Businesses located in the United States

You can create personas over time for the buyers, users, and influencers within those companies. In this example, it may include VP of customer support, CMO, CIO, customer service managers, and so on. Each one will have different priorities. After talking to a few, you'll be able to build out a persona that represents each profile including information like:

- **Personal info:** name, picture, job title, company name or type
- **Demographic info:** age, gender, income, location, education level, family info
- **Need info:** goals or primary values, primary challenges
- **Other info:** hobbies, technical capabilities, communication preferences, media habits, or any other potentially useful info

If you have an early customer or someone you've interviewed who you believe is a great representation of your target, you can use their real profile. Some people prefer this approach to creating a fake persona.

The ICP characteristics vary based on the target buyer—a consumer ICP is a little different because it will be the individual and include demographics, psychographics, socioeconomic info, brand affinity, and any other characteristics that may impact their purchase decisions.

These personas can be rough or as detailed as you are able to make them based on your knowledge. This is an iterative process to help you answer key questions about your offering and define hypotheses to test your sales motion and marketing messages. Don't spend too much time on it. Don't hire consultant. Just use it as a way to track what you learn and help your decision-making.

Getting Started with Positioning and Messaging

Even at the early part of this stage, you need a way to communicate the value of what you are offering to bring in early customers. You will need to position your offering so they understand it. The output may take many forms—a tagline, an elevator pitch—but a good place to start is a basic positioning statement:

For [*target customer*] who [*the need or opportunity*],

the [*product name*] is a [*product category*] that [*key benefit*].

Unlike [*primary competitive alternative*], our product [*primary differentiation*].

Your positioning statement should be unique, believable, and important to customers. If your team can agree on this statement, consider it a win. Then you can build out the rest of your messaging from that start.

Enterprise SaaS investor and advisor Judy Loehr recommends building out your positioning and your story more fully. She explains positioning as "how you tell the story of your company. It's how you talk about your company in a way that is compelling, authentic, and people will care about." And it will help align your team. It will most certainly need to be validated and evolve, but it is an important part of establishing product/market fit. Judy's advice:

Write it as a story: Your positioning is how you talk about your company in a way that is compelling, authentic, and people will care about. It is a very structured story flow that starts with your audience, your customers, and your prospects. It starts with their needs and the pressures going on in their companies and their market. It talks about their challenges, flows through and frames the ideal—what would their nirvana product or nirvana world look like—and takes them through a journey, where the answer at the very end might be "Hey, we do solve that problem and we solve it magically." It's a foundational piece of building a company.

Connect the dots: Positioning is like connect the dots. You need the fewest number of dots to the most compelling answer. So, being authentic, it's this is who you are, these are your challenges, this is your opportunity. We are one solution. Just boom, boom, boom, a straight shot. If the trail meanders too much, you lose everybody.

Focus on the customer, not your product and technology: Everybody starts off talking about their product and technology, and it is as boring and mind-numbing as if I walked up to you at a party and started telling you about my belly button.

Focus on the customer's pain and needs, as opposed to focusing on what you do.

Be authentic, avoid copycat messaging: Copycat messaging is where you hear really strong messaging from somebody else, and you just copy the metaphor and apply it to yourself. A lot of people are talking about the Zuora subscription economy messaging, and that it works and resonates for their audience and for their market. And it is causing a lot of other companies to use fill-in-the-blank economy messaging. Yet, if you look at them or think about them for a second, they're not about economies at all. They're not about how people or businesses or consumers pay for something. They're really not related to economies at all. And so, it just ends up being confusing. It doesn't land. It doesn't resonate. While it might work for one company, copy and pasting to yours is just not the same, it's not authentic, and you're going to have all the downstream problems, as if you just didn't do your own positioning, because you haven't.

Align on your positioning before hiring marketers to develop collateral: Do your positioning in boring black-and-white Word docs, not shiny PowerPoint presentations, because the prettiness can obfuscate the fact that the story doesn't have legs and all the pieces fleshed out. I always recommend figuring out your positioning, spending the time just on that, and when you have an end-to-end structured narrative and structured product positioning in a boring black-and-white Word doc that everyone—all the founders, the product team, the sales team, the marketing team, everybody—can look at that and go, "Yeah. That's it. That's exactly what we're doing. That's why we're all here." When everybody agrees [that] this is it and feels that it is compelling, then that is your positioning foundation that a marketing team can go forward and be successful with. Without that, everything is harder. And until you have done that, you

> might all think you're aligned, but product may be off building the product one way, while sales is talking about it just a tiny bit differently, but close enough, and marketing thinks they're going off and trying to reach a slightly different audience. That incremental lack of alignment across all those teams can be fatal for an early-stage company.

You can hire a consultant to facilitate this process if need be, but no one can do your positioning for you. Your core team needs to be engaged in the process and bought in to the final product. Without alignment on the value proposition, features, and benefits that differentiate your product and speak to your buyers and users, it's a hopeless task trying to agree on the right customer-facing copy within your company, and the various parts of your business will inevitably head in different directions.

It is easy to test and validate your messaging in surveys or in live-use cases. Test and validate your value proposition and messaging as you engage with buyers—in sales calls, emails (subject lines or content), or even through digital testing (SEM, LinkedIn or Facebook ads, landing pages, etc.). You can use A/B testing, where you test two options against each other, for more than just testing web pages. With the number of digital channels and targeting available, you can test virtually any type of content quickly and get real buyer feedback.

Your First Sales Tools

General wisdom advises you not to invest significantly in marketing at this stage. To prove the market, you have to sell, and to sell, you have to find customers. This means you have to do some marketing. It doesn't mean that you have to spend a lot, but it does mean that you have to do some work.

Your website will likely be the first important sales tool leveraging your messaging and representing your brand. The other marketing and sales tools you need will depend on your business, market, cost, and sales motion or method.

There is a tendency at this stage to go overboard on your web presence and overinvest in the first launch versus ongoing updates. Keep in mind that most organizations will evolve their fit in the market and messaging during this stage.

Optimizing for speed to market and flexibility in the website will yield more than delivering a resource-intensive, hard-to-maintain website. When in doubt, keep it simple and don't invest in anything you can't change later. One company used their early funding to invest in an expensive, time-intensive custom photo shoot to create unique personalities to display on their website—only to jettison all of those images when they updated market positioning and website a few months later.

Today's buyer is more informed than ever, and almost half of buyers identify specific solutions before even engaging with reps.[9] Whether you are marketing to small businesses or enterprises, your buyer may know a lot about the market and your competitors before they engage with your website, and they will have high expectations for the content they'll find there.

If you are targeting enterprises, you probably will have a high-touch sales process where your founder or sales rep is personally meeting with sales prospects. In addition to your website, you may need sales presentations, demos, one pagers, or brochures. If you are targeting smaller business, buyers may conduct even more of the sales cycle independently—through tools as simple as search, industry analysis, end-user review sites, influencer blogs and social, or other digital channels. This will likely again be different for marketplaces or consumer businesses, and so on.

There is no cookbook, no one-size-fits-all solution. Start with your customer—how they become aware and learn new solutions, how they conduct their evaluation process (who they trust, what channels they use, etc.). Define your concept of "sales tools" broadly based on how your buyer prefers to engage with new solutions, and consider both the internal- and external-facing resources that will accelerate velocity through the sales cycle.

Another important—and often overlooked—area is defining the post-sales process. You may put your product manager or customer success team on point for adoption and satisfaction, but marketing can help automate and scale customer programs. Content and tools for onboarding new customers and driving adoption of new features are areas that marketing can support

---

9   "Study: Half of B2B Buyers Make Up Their Minds before Talking to Sales Reps," Miller Heiman Group, June 5, 2018, https://www.millerheimangroup.com/press-release/study-half-of-b2b-buyers-make-up-their-minds-before-talking-to-sales-reps.

with email, videos, websites, and so on. It is much more cost-effective to retain (and expand) than to acquire new customers. And converting these early customers into loyal advocates who drive organic growth for your business will be invaluable.

Start with a hypothesis on the top sales content and tools critical to educating your buyers during the sales cycle and driving adoption post-sale. Then, use feedback from sales and customer success (as well as buyer engagement and usage data) to understand how your specific buyers are responding and using that content. And then iterate.

- What channels are working to reach prospects? Which prospects?
- What messages are working in those channels? Which are not?
- What sales decks are effective? What points are raising objections?
- What is causing friction in the sales process? In customer adoption?

Though you are likely focused around getting the product right, you can learn a lot from these early sales and marketing experiments. Treat these sales engagements just as you are treating your product prototypes and versions, as opportunities to test and validate.

Beginning to Reach the Market

Beyond your website, content can be a great way to test the market's interest and build inbound traffic. The value of content, particularly for explaining new categories, was echoed by many founders we spoke to. There are many different approaches, depending on your product and market, but this can be a great tactic to start early.

Erik Larson says this about using content to aid in category creation:

> We've always invested in content marketing because we keep learning interesting things. One of our hypotheses is that what we're all working on is inherently interesting and that's a strategic advantage in the software market. It helps that potential buyers and influencers are fascinated by the topic.
>
> It's also important because what we're working on is a new idea—that there can be software to help you track and im-

prove decisions. That's a new thing. So we have to tell the story and do it in a scalable way.

Stacey Epstein says this about creating a channel to reach the market at ServiceMax:

> When I joined ServiceMax, which was focused on field service in specific industries, there was no established community. There was one publication that nobody read. I was like, "Where are they? So I can market. Oh, they're nowhere. They don't even talk to each other. They're in their garage fixing something. They're not at a show like an HR person, right?"
>
> We had to create the community ourselves. We created our own content site that we called Field Service Digital. Actually, in the early days we called it Smart Band until we could buy the URL Field Service Digital. And we created a content site. And we pumped articles. It was not affiliated with ServiceMax. We pumped it with articles. And we just put it out to the community. Then we started having events.
>
> Sometimes you have the luxury of a big, horizontal market, and you can spray and pray, and it works. And sometimes you are selling to a very narrow market. But it worked. ServiceMax dominates that space now.

Jon Miller says this about standing out with thought leadership:

> There's so much content out there today that its important for people to really make the super-high-quality stuff that stands out. Multiple times I've had success writing the "definitive book" on the topic around our space and used that thought leadership to help create our brand, create our awareness, and to create leads.
>
> At Engagio, I wrote the complete guide to account-based marketing. And I started working on that before

we even had product because I really wanted to establish that thought leadership position for our company.

I'm also a big fan of partner marketing for driving demand, where you work with other companies that sell to a similar audience but don't compete with you and ride on each other's awareness and build that mutually. In the early days at Engagio, I did a lot of webinars with partners where we both promoted the webinar and shared the registrant lists. That was a really good, very low-cost way to start to build out our database of contacts. The content and the partner marketing strategies work together, in that we talked about the thought leadership from the book on these webinars.

One great trick here, especially for organizations with limited resources, is to think about the Thanksgiving turkey example originated by analyst Rebecca Lieb, formerly at Altimeter:

Think of your content like the turkey at Thanksgiving. You have your big meal on Thursday, and then maybe a snack of it that night. You make a turkey sandwich on Friday, turkey soup on Saturday, and then a pot pie on Sunday. That same turkey feeds you in different ways for three or four days. Same with your content. Too many companies create a great piece of content and feed their customer just one time with it. But you can get so much more out of it. Record your speaking event and turn that into several 30-second videos. Make your webinar into a series of social posts and a blog. No matter what you do, always be thinking of the way you can get another meal out of your content.

A common mistake is to publish an article or a webinar or a white paper or other content and move on. Look for ways to publish that content in other forms and on multiple platforms. Think about how many emails, invitations to webinars, and content you see on your daily basis—in your inbox, on social, and so on.

Breaking through the noise requires dedicated effort and meeting your prospects when they are ready to engage and in their preferred channel. Remember, some people enjoy the Thanksgiving leftovers more than the actual turkey.

Initially, you may start getting content out to learn, but you'll want to start measuring it's impact to see what is working. Emilia Chagas, CEO of Contentools.com, advises:

> You should always measure content in terms of revenue. How much of your revenue is coming from the content that you're deploying? How many people are coming to your website? And how many of those people are converting to leads, maybe subscribing to a newsletter? How many of them are following your drip campaigns and requesting demos, are actually buying your products, and are coming back to buy more?

Margaret Molloy, Global Chief Marketing Officer, Siegel+Gale on "What Is Brand"

Brand is a strategic asset. It includes the customer experience, our values, our purpose, the problem we're solving in the world, why we exist, why should someone care if we go away next week, through to what is our name. All of these dimensions make brand a vitally important investment of time and resource.

From day one, founders should be thinking about purpose. What's our company's purpose, our meaning? Your purpose impacts product, but it also impacts your ability to hire engineers and bring on investors, as well as customers.

Founders should also be thinking about their visual identity. How do we show up? What do we look like? Everything from the choice of color palettes through to typography and to all the artifacts that go with a brand signal something. Making sure there's coherence between where they're going and what these assets are signaling is important.

Now there are practical matters—product needs to get out, stuff needs to get done—but having brand as an item on that checklist to think about is vitally important. It even impacts the product—is there a product interface? That is a brand touch point, the user experience. Brand is the holistic set of experiences a constituent has with your entity, so what is the brand experience? Are we simple? Are we whimsical? Are we serious? All of these qualities need to be deliberate, and there's no one answer that's better than another; it just needs to be consistent across every touch point.

The Marketing Team at This Stage

"The biggest mistake companies can possibly make is to start hiring a go-to-market team before they're ready," advises Bruce Cleveland. We heard from many investors and founders in our interviews that one of the most common mistakes they see is overinvestment in marketing and the marketing organization prior to product/market fit. This is a tricky balance, because at least some marketing is necessary for most companies to get to product/market fit. But companies that invest and try to scale too early often crash and burn as they run out of money.

This is the stage when you will need your first marketing hire. Your early marketer should be a utility player, someone with some experience who can jump in and figure out how to do anything that comes their way. Marketing is pretty broad, there are many different domains and skill sets in marketing, and though they may overlap, you won't find anyone who is an expert or even strong in them all. Determine who to hire based on your target market and go-to-market approach, your assessment of your team's strengths and gaps, and what you think you'll need to focus on in the near term. But make sure they aren't too narrow and are open and excited about learning new things. You'll want to hire someone who has those skills, is adaptable, and can do what you need today and figure out the other pieces.

As a founder, you need to hire this initial person (or team) and work closely with them to ensure that they have fully internalized your mission, vision, and market fit so that they are developing programs and activities that map to these goals. Seldom does a founder turn their back on marketing with this first hire, but make sure that you are partnering with and fostering this first group of people.

For B2B companies, a product marketer is often a great first hire. Many startups think demand generation for their first hire. You will definitely need demand generation expertise as you get some traction and move into really testing channels and growth mode. The challenge with starting with a demand generation person is they need content and messaging to make their programs work. Without strong messaging and content, demand generation programs will fail.

Folia Grace, VP of marketing for Talkdesk, says:

> You can outsource creation of demand generation programs. There's tons of agencies that do that. You can even outsource setting up a Marketo merge or whatever. But it's very hard to find somebody external that understands your product and your buyer or that can go talk to analysts and really develop your story, your pitch.
>
> So it's never too early to bring in someone to understand the buyer and build your pitch. You can almost do that at the beginning stages of your company once you have enough funding and enough traction that you know you've got something built to begin with.

Greg Powell recommends hiring a product marketer as your first hire for B2B companies:

> Depending on the company and the founder's skill set or the PM's skill set, product marketing can be a really good first marketing hire. I've seen engineers and even PMs get caught up in solving technical problems and lose sight of the audience that might use that technology. I think about a product marketer as thinking from the outside in and providing that healthy skepticism to say, "All right, but who's going to buy this thing?"
>
> If you're building a product for enterprises, product marketing is a really good first marketing hire because the story becomes crucial for the sales team to sell to potential customers. The product marketer can build that deck, the story, and the content that the salespeople can use and get that story in front of the right people and sell that story and sell the product.
>
> For consumer-oriented products it's a little different. You

tend to have a couple different scenarios. One is the virtuous cycle built from virality from the product, like a social network product. SEM and SEO could be your best first marketing hires, and product marketing can come later. There, a small SEM budget can go a long way in figuring out what works. Same thing with SEO, where you can just get your name out there. And that can be a more effective way to start understanding the product/market fit for a consumer-oriented company.

In general, your first marketer will need to at least be able to write, develop messaging, create presentations, and execute some demand generation programs. You can fill in any gaps with freelancers and agencies.

Technology Investments at This Stage

It's too early to make big investments in marketing technology at this stage, before you know your sales motion and go-to-market strategy. Definitely don't make any large long-term investments. But monthly or annual subscriptions to software for managing your website and, for B2B, an easy CRM solution for tracking prospects and customers are useful investments. You can buy these separately or choose combined solutions like Hubspot and others that have both and enable you to easily add landing pages for campaigns and track the generated leads. The ability of your marketing team to get pages up quickly and change messaging and designs without engineering help will be essential, especially as you move into the next stage. And you need your engineers focused on building product, not tweaking your website.

The CRM investment will enable you to track your early sales pipeline and learnings to align your leadership team and ensure you are focused on the right priorities.

Startup marketing leader Anita Pandey explains:

> Pipeline management and integrity is critical. Are you losing deals to your competition or because of product gaps? Are you focusing on the wrong customer? Starting to track your pipeline

early builds a closed feedback loop between product, marketing, and sales; it begins to create a metrics oriented culture; and it helps align your leadership.

Just Do Something

Whatever you do with respect to marketing, do something. Try something. Experiment somewhere. These trials will provide a foundation that you can build on later, either by learning what doesn't work or by building on and leveraging what does.

Kate Bradley Chernis says:

> One of the most important things you can do as a startup is to get some baseline so that when you do have the money or the people power to put more in to it, you have something to work with. That's so helpful as opposed to starting with that blank slate. It doesn't matter even if it's just the littlest amount. We gave our CMO a huge gift when he walked in because he saw, "Oh wow, you've been doing this for a year," We had a 56% organic traffic rate, just because we were doing it. I wasn't able to convert that into anything because I didn't have the man-power to do it, but he was able to walk in and build something from it.
>
> Don't get overwhelmed with all the channels. Just do one thing, try to be as good as you can, do your best at that, focus on that, then worry about the other stuff later.

Moving Forward

The quest for product/market fit most certainly has a crucial product piece to it. But the market piece is the yin to its yang. Both parts are needed to reach that elusive goal. There are critical go-to-market aspects that, if done at this stage, can set you up for future success (or failure if not tackled early). Clearly defining that customer and understanding why they buy is at the core. From there you can derive the channels to reach them, messaging to engage, their willingness to pay, and more. A first marketing generalist or product marketer can help you nail these pieces and develop those early sales tools to help you close deals.

5

PROVE THE BUSINESS

The looming question at this stage:

- I'm ready to turn on marketing; what should I do first?

This chapter will cover:

- Starting to build your marketing team
- Determining the right investments
- Developing a marketing playbook

Silicon Valley is filled with growth-focused organizations. This stage can be wickedly challenging for organizations as pressures mount to go, go, grow! Todd worked with one organization for a consumer services application in the travel and transportation industry. They had done a fair job—quick and dirty, but reliable—of discovering their target market and had a product that had the potential to be unique in the space. The pressure was on to jump off the cliff and start running marketing programs. The leadership agreed to test some messages and some channels to match the issue they were solving with the potential buyer and where they might best connect with that buyer. In retrospect, the perspective of the CEO was "I have a great product that solves a problem. Why aren't we just minting money?"

They never fully achieved high growth because there was never any opportunity to test and try and make mistakes they could learn from. So they never really understood where travel administrators in small to medium businesses in manufacturing might hang out or gather information, what would capture their attention, or what would get them to try the service or advocate with their bosses to try it.

Knowing who you want to talk to is only part of the battle.

As you are entering this stage, you should have a product or service and you should have customers who are willing to buy it. You should have some level of confidence—if not validation—of what you are doing in the market. You should have a sense of where your market is and some ideas about who the customers are in that market. The urge will be to step on the gas and go full steam ahead toward that market.

If you are like most business leaders, none of this is going as quickly as you would like it. You have this amazing idea that can change the world or, at least, your corner of it. You have built this great product or service, so the idea of waiting is painful. There are also natural pressures from advisors or investors to move quickly. You have probably read some stories about unicorn companies who had phenomenal successes, seemingly overnight. Your impulse will be to go all in now and push forward to get your marketing engine running and to start acquiring customers and getting them to buy.

Let's go, already!

But it is good to take stock of where you are right now. You have a great product or service, or one that is certainly on the right path to being great. You know who your customer is and you have a sense of the market you want to address. You have a few customers who are using your product and are delighted by your organization and the value you ultimately provide. But what you don't have is revenue. You then find yourself in one of three typical camps: you are bootstrapping, so you have little money to waste; you have some investment with little money to waste; or you have ample resources with which to acquire customers as quickly as possible. If you are in one of the first two camps, making a big gamble on marketing in the hopes that you get lucky on the strategy that works is a risky bet. If you are on a run to acquire customers, know that companies like Fab and Evernote (and many others) went on spending sprees and had high burn rates, which ultimately sank or shrunk the company's bigger ambitions. As Marc Andreessen of Andreessen Horowitz tweeted: "High burn rate kills your ability to adapt as you learn & market changes. Co becomes unwieldy, too big to easily change course."

Jumping off the cliff and building the hang glider on the way down is a thrill. But you can still have aggressive growth—in fact, even more aggressive growth—by making sure you are finding the best path forward. But wasting money for the sake of feeling like you are moving forward might be one of the bigger mistakes you can make.

This chapter will discuss how to move forward and set yourself up for exponential growth, while avoiding some of the traps and pitfalls others have readily jumped into. This chapter is reminiscent of the tortoise and the hare. Going full speed may feel like the best and fastest approach to your goals, but we have seen too many instances of organizations who stepped on the marketing gas too early (even too recklessly) only to burn limited resources and time and miss the customer entirely. If you feel confident at some point that going fast is the correct action, then be your best counsel and make that leap. We recommend the "slow and steady wins the race" approach at this stage to keep moving forward but in a way that helps get you to your goal but with reduced risk, churn, or resource burn.

Focus of This Stage

You know who your potential customer is, and you have a product that they want. This was the work you did to establish the product/market fit in the prior chapter. But what are the most effective ways to reach this customer, which messages will catch their attention, and when? There is a reason that TV in the wee hours of Saturday and Sunday morning is saturated with "getting in shape" and health-related advertising. P90X and a few other brands' studies have shown that their buyer is the person sleeping on the couch or just waking up from a night of indulgence and are motivated to make a change and to purchase.

At this stage, your energies should be spent on developing a playbook of repeatable programs that get the best message to the customer through the best channel and at the best time. The programs should be is coordinated with other marketing efforts, and have outcomes that you can measure to know—not feel, not guess, but know—which programs are working and which ones should change.

This is about testing and repeatability. If you skip this step and rush to market, you may get lucky and hit upon that one program that works, but you are more likely to waste your limited marketing resources on programs and activities that don't work. When that happens, most leaders then turn their attention to the teams who have failed, churning good people and rebuilding their teams. This can cause months of delay in getting your product to market. We have seen organizations repeat this "go, go, go" mentality through two or three refreshed marketing organizations, only to come to the conclusion that marketing doesn't work for their organization.

However, if you can test and iterate at this stage, you can more quickly develop a repeatable playbook of campaigns and programs that will drive your business faster and further and reduce your resource costs.

How you prove the business and prepare yourself for that rapid growth will be different for consumer sales, small to medium businesses, or enterprises. How you go to market for a purely digital sale will be very different than if you are selling into enterprise business. Big elephant hunting for a few large deals will require a different strategy than selling to a mass market. We will walk through how these strategies are managed at this stage and how you can still grow the business while developing your go-to-market playbook.

Because this step is so important, we will share a few examples of where this failed for organizations.

One organization that was selling to the enterprise space was sure of who their buyer was. They knew what type of company to target and what role they needed to sell to within that organization. They felt their product was world-class and a real game changer for the market—a unicorn in the making. Eager to move forward, they hired a sizeable outside sales organization and crafted regions for them to manage. They hired an inside sales organization to manage first contacts with the customer and prioritize those customers for the sales team. Because their competitors were heavily invested in trade shows and events, they invested heavily on events, oftentimes 12 months in advance, to secure prime floor space.

They did not invest in marketing. The team was minimal and the budget small. The belief was that the product was such a game changer that the sales organization could successfully explain the value to the customer and that marketing was unnecessary.

The problems started to arise when the leads did not come into the sales organization. And what leads did come were of poor quality. The inside sales organization did not have scripts to work from, so each person developed their own approach, with their own message and their own style. So even when a lead was passed to the sales team, the expectations of the customers were so wildly different that the sales team had to waste time and energy setting expectations with the customer and failed to establish rapport.

The event strategy failed because they were following the lead of their competitors. Furthermore, as a disrupter in the space, their buyer was not at the trade shows and events—the competitors' buyer was there. Few leads ever came from the shows.

Salespeople will naturally follow the money, so the good ones left quickly. Morale was low, and it permeated the entire organization, causing doubt across the company if this product was ever going to be as successful as they had hoped.

Conversely, another organization believed in marketing and had a generous percentage of their budget allocated to the marketing team. They hired top talent and empowered them to run programs. Their model was consumer focused and transacted through digital web sales. The customer purchased online. They had a great product and a marketplace that could use it. The leadership adopted a "go and grow" mentality.

The marketing team rushed forward and executed brilliantly but without a strategy. Beautiful campaigns were created, and they saturated barren markets. Great messages were crafted, but they missed the intended buyer. Meanwhile, new emerging markets, industries, and geographies were not being given adequate marketing attention.

The marketing team that was hired had a certain expertise and a bias toward certain markets and marketing in certain ways. Without proper guidance and direction, they went to their comfort zone. With high expectations and a budget to match, they spent a lot of money going to that comfort zone, but that was not where their customer was or where the customer could experience the brand.

Both situations resulted in a ton of finger pointing and blame, which led to even more distraction and a loss of progress in taking these amazing products to market. And while it is often easy to ignore the soft costs of these failures, morale and culture had profound impact across the organization. Finance, operations, engineering, customer service, and so on all saw what was happening and started to become demoralized. Many became unwilling to explore new approaches in their organization—to try something new or make suggestions for improvements. It became toxic. The belief—even if never fully articulated or fully conscious—was that if you take risks, even calculated risks, and they don't yield results, you are thrown under the bus.

Both organizations failed in their go-to-market strategy. One underinvested, and the other overinvested. But both failed to take a strategic approach to how they would connect the customer to their product.

The focus should be on testing and iteration. Successful testing is about placing small bets across a variety of marketing channels, with different messages, at different times, and in different formats. The video you create on Facebook may underperform during the weekday but may exceed expectations on the weekends. The message you deliver on your blog may only get family members to read it, but suddenly goes viral when you deliver it on YouTube. That all-important feature of your product that you think will cause it to fly off the shelves may not be of interest to your buyer, but if messaged a different way may suddenly motivate them in unexpected ways.

Message, channel, format, saturation, the number of exposures to the message, date, time—all of these variables help you connect with your customer. But if you don't deliver the message at the right time and in the right place and in the right way, the customer won't connect. It is never as simple as "I want this customer; now go market to them."

This becomes even more complex if you are thinking about changes in industry, company decision makers, geography (do people in Italy buy differently than those in France?), seasonality, and so on. Do you have multiple versions of the product that appeal to different buyers? Are they buying on a mobile device or desktop? Will what works today work tomorrow? What failed—even miserably—yesterday may be a huge success tomorrow. The calculations here are complex and change as customer behaviors change or morph and as new competition enters the market. Some external factor may throw your best plans either into or out of alignment.

Small bets, placed systematically and strategically across all of these variables, will yield mostly failures. However, it will identify the successes. These become your playbook and will allow you to enter the next phase, scaling for success.

The Customer Journey

As you think about focusing your energies on acquiring customers, it is time to start thinking of the customer beyond the acquisition—to think of their entire interactions with your organization. Most leaders still think of the customer as something to acquire, that you get the customer and then you're on to the next customer. This notion of a pipeline is firmly rooted in the minds of many business leaders, salespeople, and marketers.

Start thinking of how to engage your customer based on their understanding of you. Do they know you already, or are they hearing about you for the first time? Do they recognize you? Do they understand you? Are they thinking about how you might be a solution to their problem? The decision to purchase may be instantaneous, or it may only be after they have seen you multiple times that they finally engage with you.

So, not only do you have to know how to reach your customer, but you need to know what they know or feel about you when you do that. To further complicate this, it starts to become a circular relationship as loyal—or unsatisfied—customers impact how you are perceived in the market. How many of your personal buying decisions have been influenced by a disparaging comment made about a brand by a friend, or by positive reviews online?

Experimentation

At this stage you and your marketers should be on a path to investigate what will work best to draw in your customer. It is not blindly trying; it is systematic and rigorous. And it starts with a hypothesis.

If you did the work in the prior chapter, you have a good idea of your product/market fit. You know what value your product has in the market and what your customer looks like. This is a great place to start. Unless you have some data that strongly points you in a certain direction, your first step on the path of testing may be intuition.

Let's pause on this idea. Most leaders are uncomfortable with marketing by intuition. One of the great advances in marketing is that so much of it is digital and, as a result, so much of it can be measured. But this change has also caused one of marketing's greatest challenges. Business leaders expect marketing to be data driven and known. However, unless you have heavily invested in market research or earlier experimentation, you are going to need to test and iterate at this stage. This means making the smartest bet you can make with the best available data—and still realizing that many of these bets will fail. The failures of these tests should be funded and accounted for not as failures but as important learnings that will drive success.

When Jill joined Freshworks (previously Freshdesk), they faced a challenge of building their brand and growing market share in the US. One program they tested was in-person thought leadership events to improve brand perception and generate leads. The idea was based on the insight that customer service leaders lacked a good community for sharing challenges and learnings and that this was a group that would welcome such a thing. They hired an agency to plan and execute the pilot event and focused on proving it out and learning. It wasn't a slam dunk immediately, but that first event was successful enough, measured in leads and positive feedback from attendees, that they expanded the series globally, experimenting with different formats, types of locations, and times of day for their different markets and evolved the program over time. For this business and market, that program worked. (In fact, it worked so well for Freshworks that competitors launched similar programs.)

Channels and Personas

Start a strategy session with your marketing team to understand what you know about your customer and their need for the product. Many marketers will think of this in terms of persona development. What are the personas of the customers—who are they and what are they like. This can be sophisticated and can lead to backstories of what a customer may look like. Fredrick Finance, Betty Benefits, Todd Technology, Sally Sales, and so on. Persona-based marketing will help you picture what someone on the receiving end of your campaign will look and act like.

This is a valuable exercise, but it doesn't have to be arduous or time-consuming. The goal here is to have an idea of who you are communicating with, what will make them interested in your product or service, and what the thing that motivates them to buy will be.

Your product design team likely goes through a similar exercise to create user personas, but be careful of assuming you can simply use theirs, as your buyers and users may not be the same people, and you may need to include some different information. For instance, some of the people involved in purchasing and influencing the purchase of your product may not ever go near the product. The design team may not consider this user in their persona efforts. Also, their format may take a story or "jobs to be done" approach, focused on the user's intended tasks. Though this information may be useful to you, you will likely also want to include demographic, location, and other personal information as well.

This becomes the basis of your hypothesis to start testing ways to reach them. My buyer can be described as _____, they will like _____ about my product, and _____ is a good place to communicate with them. At this point, you should be able to fill out the first two spaces—you should be able to describe your customer and know what they like about your product. This is where persona work can be so informative. It allows you to make some strategic guesses about where to communicate with them.

It is important to stress that—except in rare cases—this is still a guess. Many leaders will get uncomfortable at this stage because the urge is to rush forward or to want to *know* how to best get in front of the customer. The basis of this testing phase is to get to that level of clarity.

For instance, if you are selling a revolutionary coffee maker, you may know that your buyer has disposable income to pay above-market prices for your machine, that they are technologically savvy, and that they are sophisticated and concerned with design. You may create a persona for them—even going so far as to envision them living in a loft, making a six-figure income, and being concerned about fashion and automobiles.

Given this, you might jump to a strategy that might naturally target when they consume coffee: an ad campaign that focuses on early-morning banner ads on social media. That approach may be successful and is worth trying. However, brands like Chanel and Gucci have advertised in *Car and Driver* (a seemingly unintuitive place for their buyer) because they know that their buyer likes certain automobiles. When those auto brands are featured, they know their potential buyer is likely to see their ads. Spotify ran a successful 2016 billboard campaign by sifting through their data to understand exactly the mood their listeners were in and to play on that in their messaging. The direct approach may well work and work well, but by developing these personas you can oftentimes find an indirect approach that will connect you to the buyer when they are most likely to pay attention to your message.

This is why testing and investigating is so critically important.

That first hypothesis will be the basis for your testing to prove it, or to prove it wrong.

The first thing to remember when establishing a testing strategy is that not everything will work. In fact, you should go so far as to think that most things will fail. It is not a stretch to think that if 10% of your testing actually works, you are ahead of the game.

Your testing should be pragmatic and rigorous. First, start with your basic premise, your hypothesis. Your product or service will be enjoyed by a certain customer. You believe that these customers can be reached at certain times and over certain channels. For instance, if you are trying to reach CFOs, think about where finance leaders gather information. What do they read or watch? Do they belong to associations or groups? What captures their attention? If you are trying to reach millennials with a certain amount of disposable income, where do they shop or where do they visit in person or online? Since it is often a guess—even an educated one—this is why the testing is so key.

One personal example of this is Todd's career at SAP. There wasn't a CFO on the planet who had not heard of SAP—which is not a position most entrepreneurs find themselves in, having one of the best-known brands on the planet. However, SAP needed to change the mindset of the CFO as they offered new products and services. It was challenging to do at scale (versus having each salesperson try to get all of their CFO clients on the phone). Multiple messages were tested across several social media channels (Facebook, LinkedIn, Twitter), in different formats (emails, blogs, videos, papers), with all of them directed at the CFO. The results: zip, zilch, nada. It was a failure. However, Todd noticed that when educational content was developed toward CFOs' inner circle (their right-hand leader, who might be a head of accounts receivable, accounting, payroll, or tax), those people were an eager audience for the message. That was their "in" for the organization, the foot in the door. He developed videos, blogs, content that was geared toward educating these key leaders on challenges they were facing in the marketplace and how SAP was focusing on solving this issue. Suddenly, these leaders were helping to bring SAP in front of the CFO. It reopened the conversation with the CFO because the brand connected with trusted advisors who became their advocates.

Looking back, it would have been great to have the insight up front and to accelerate that entire program. SAP could have saved six months of work if they had known then what they know now. But a testing phase helps make those insights possible. By comparison, other groups were engaged in same old marketing programs, which were yielding lackluster results. This is a great A/B test: the old way of doing things yielded poor results, yet the new way—with some trial and testing—quickly yielded stellar results.

If someone said, "Go win the office of the CFO," most people would buy a list from a magazine, spend a lot of money on a conference focused on CFOs, or try to win them over by calling a few directly. Some would send a gift basket or a package of goodies to make the customer feel obligated to take the pursuing phone call. If these are all you try, you may get lucky, but you will probably miss less obvious opportunities that open up new doors for your conversation.

Are you building your organization on the hope that luck will be in your favor?

Measurement: Think of the Outcome and Work Backward

One company we knew was buying email lists to acquire customers. They would acquire a list for $5,000, blast a few emails, and measured that two customers came onboard. A typical customer deal was $10,000, so a fourfold return on their investment. This encouraged repeating this behavior. Then a funny thing happened: word got back from interactions with these prospects that most people were turned off by the messages or thought that the product wasn't for them. The list buying and emails were suspended, and the message was reworked. With better customer insight, the emails started again and yielded 13–20 customers per list. The two customers seemed like they were wins until they realized they were leaving customers on the table.

Instead of randomly trying different approaches, think about what you want to happen at each stage. Do you want the buyer to simply be aware of your brand or product? Are you trying to motivate the buyer to learn more about you? Do you want to lead them to make a purchase? Think about what you want them to do, then start thinking about how you are going to measure success. You should start with your measurement first. "I want the buyer to click our 'learn more' button." "I want the buyer to read the blog." "I want the buyer to subscribe." "I want the revenue!"

An old saying goes, not everything that counts can be counted, and not everything that can be counted counts.

You may want to measure some behavior and believe that you should be able to collect data on that behavior, but not everything you want is measurable. Some of these measurements may be anecdotal; some may be based on limited analytic insights. It is important to know that up front. Contrary to what some people will tell you, just because so much of marketing is digital, it doesn't mean that you can measure every interaction. Or that you should. Or that all data is insightful.

For instance, say a customer clicks a link to have a salesperson call them or finally buys a pair of those shoes online. Was it that click that deserves the credit or the blog they read last week or the 21 preceding ads they saw but didn't react to. Was it the conversation they had with a friend the day before, or the event where they walked by your booth two months earlier? Last-touch attribution refers to assigning the last thing a customer did before the purchase as the motivator to buy. Most know that purchasing is not that simple and that last touch would probably have failed had it not been for the prior interactions you had with the customer.

Some of your measurements may be purely anecdotal. It may be collecting some random pieces of information that further your understanding of what is working or not working. For instance, for the SAP CFO example, part of what told them it was working was people coming up to them at trade shows and recognizing us from the videos we had created. Hearing "You're the guy in the video!" five or six times started to tell them that there was something there worth exploring.

The goal here is to know what you are measuring and how you plan to measure it—even if that measurement is sometimes fuzzy. The best way to think of this is to work backward. Most measuring is done at the end of the program—it is something that is tacked onto the end of planning for a program. However, if you work backward and determine what you want to understand or what result you want to have, you can evolve that thinking against what is measurable. You may want to know what they last three websites visited by that prospect who finally comes to your website, but that may not be available. So evolve your thinking to ask:

- What is our goal? What do we wish to understand?
- What can we measure today?
- What could we measure, and what will it take to do that?
- What is not measurable today (that we would like to know)?
- What is our comfort level for making assumptions or being in a gray area of data?

A/B and Multivariate Testing

Starting with your premise and what you want to accomplish, you can now start trying different combinations. You may feel comfortable about your message, so you experiment with delivering that message across a variety of channels. That message is posted on your blog or social media channels, delivered on LinkedIn and Facebook, hung on your booth or a billboard or a side of a bus or at gate 62 at SFO.

You may want to know when your audience is online, so you test delivering it at certain times. For years, brands would message to business people during the work week, until a few organizations started testing weekend times, finding there was less noise and distraction, and that business leaders were more engaged on the weekends when they weren't so focused on their work.

You may find that it is only after seeing the ad seven times that the engagement goes up dramatically.

That viral video that everyone is after may not work for you, but a sponsored video ad on Facebook might work really well. That sponsored post in a very specific trade magazine may do better than the brief mention of the company name in the *Wall Street Journal*.

Testing Is Small Bets

There are so many variables in getting your message to the right people. You can hedge a few bets by knowing your customer and knowing what your product can deliver. You can start with some assumptions and be rational about your decisions. But this is a time for small bets placed across a variety of sites, channels, experiences, messages, and formats.

If you go big on any one, you miss knowing what might work really well in other combinations. Even if the one combination you try feels like it is working, you might find 10 times the results by changing one small thing.

Part of the reason to test is that you discover what your edges of success are. You may think something is working, but testing will help you know. It will help you make sure that your efforts are yielding your best results.

Also, it is inevitably true that what works today won't work tomorrow. Testing will help you know when results are slipping and when it is time to try new techniques or reinvestigate old ones. What works today won't work forever, so keep checking in on how your results are trending.

This is why this testing phase is so critical.

Mike Moran, Former Distinguished Engineer at IBM and Now President of The Mike Moran Group, a Consultancy Specializing in Data and AI for Organizations, on Using Data in Decision-Making

One thing I see in small companies and big companies alike is that there is a certain mindset that creeps in at times where people feel they can't make data-driven decisions because the data isn't that good, and therefore they really have to make the data a lot better before they can start making the decisions. And until then, they are really going to just go with their guts for decisions. That's actually the worst thing that you can do. And it's not because everybody has bad judgment; it's because your judgment probably doesn't get much better faster, and your judgment doesn't scale.

If you are trying to grow, you need to have a way of making decisions that scale. However, you are better off using data to make a wrong decision than you are using your judgment to make a right decision. Let me say that again: you are better off using data to make a wrong decision than you are using your judgment to make a right decision. Here is the reason why: If you used your judgment, you may get it right, or you may get it wrong. But if you used data to make a decision and you make a wrong decision, you are motivated to fix that data.

If you don't use the data for decision-making, there is no motivation to fix the data. There's no motivation to make that data better. So I will argue that the way to get your data to be better is to start making decisions on it—and if it makes everyone queasy to do that, then you are going to focus really hard on making that data better and better and better. Because there is no reason to invest in data if you aren't going to make decisions with it.

Start the change in your culture first, make the decision to use data, and you will find there will be no end of people interested in making investments to make the data better and better. That is the key: act first, and then you'll get your confidence about it later. If you wait until you have confidence in your data, it is going to take forever to get the improvements and the data that you need before you feel comfortable. It's not about being comfortable. This is about developing a system that makes itself improve and lets you scale.

Developing a Playbook

Your goal through this process is to develop a playbook of what is working to reach your market. You want to know across the formula what is the best combination of pieces to have a working campaign. It doesn't have to be perfect, and there still may be a variable or two that you may not have fully cracked the code on to know exactly what works, but you have a good idea of the messages and channels and when or how often to deliver the campaign. You'll want to exit this stage with proof that you can scale up this business and a clear idea of what you'll need to invest where to traverse the heel of the hockey stick and start scaling.

For instance, you may know that your key message works best in video format and your best times to broadcast are on the weekends, or that sponsored blog posts across several mainstream media sites work best during the week. You may be all about Facebook advertising or find that great images on Pinterest really drive you to new customers.

Once you know what things work, this is when you are ready to start moving to the next phase, where you can scale for rapid growth. This is where you develop your playbook. Put into very tactical terms, you start to develop a library of assets (videos, blogs, landing pages, banners, photography, etc.) and a sense of how to assemble them to drive customer behaviors. This can be as simple or sophisticated as you need it to be. We have seen some brands have these on a shared drive folder with one person who pulls them together to execute the campaign. Others have used sophisticated campaign management solutions to run these programs, with both in-house and external teams that deliver against a rigorous timeline to deliver these programs.

It is critical that the organization adopt a formula with enough information (read: data) that allows you to start putting real money behind these programs. One way to test if you ready to move to the next steps and start growing at scale is to justify the playbook across senior leadership or key stakeholders.

This can be as simple or sophisticated as you like it, but take your playbook and the key findings of your testing and justify your approach with key leadership. One very direct method we have used is, at a board meeting or with the leadership team, walk them through the hypothesis and why it was chosen, all the way through all of the variables tested, and why you have come to the conclusion that this is the playbook you will use moving forward.

Many leaders may skip this step, but remember that everyone in your organization believes themselves to be a marketer. Sooner or later, someone in another division will say, "My friend at company so-and-so had great success marketing to their customers in this way. Why aren't we doing that?" Or "At my last company we...." Or "Our competitor is all over this; why aren't we?" It is in the team's best interest share with the key stakeholders what has been tested, what failed, what worked, and why.

Casey Winter, Growth Advisor at Greylock Partners: Build Up and from Within

Traditionally what entrepreneurs at that stage have done is they've tried to go hire an exec to figure it out, like hire a VP in marketing. And that usually doesn't work out so well because most of the time, you are hiring an exec from a company much larger than you are, and you think they are going to bring the best practices to your company. But really, they are bringing the best practices of a much larger company. They are not bringing the best practices to a company at your stage, so they try to hire too many people. You don't see the results very quickly. And as an entrepreneur, you're like, what's going on? Like all of a sudden, I've got 10 people over here, I am still not growing any faster. And then, that's why you see a lot of VP of marketing with fairly short tenures.

What I've seen the smarter entrepreneurs do—and I mean just smarter because it's worked, not that they're more intelligent or anything—is they are finding people that have been at the company for a while and have a lot of in-depth knowledge. And they're just saying, "Hey, I know you have been working on this thing. But now, actually growth is the thing I want you to work on." Marketing, sales, improving sales, improving marketing, improving the product's ability to drive more users. They just take a couple seasoned people, usually like an engineer, a designer, an early marketer, an early PM, whatever, and they just say, "Hey, go off in the corner and work on one of these pieces that is inhibiting growth." It could be the onboarding. It could be the conversion rate of a phone call to a sale. It could be the capturing of email addresses. There's just so many of these parts in a funnel that usually an early-stage startup hasn't worked on a whole lot but provides some big opportunity. And they just get a couple people, and they said, "Just go off in the corner and work exclusively on this. Run a bunch of experiments, and try to figure out what you can do."

And then, what I've seen companies does in that regard is they'll come back later, and they're like, "Yeah. We actually just doubled our conversion rate to sign-up," or to email capture. At that point, the entrepreneur is like, "Wow, this has massive impact to every metric of our business. How do I fuel this even more?" And that's usually when you start making it a bigger team, and then you start thinking about bringing in a management layer to call in a growth team, call in a marketing team, whatever the case may be.

The mistakes I've seen is people try to hire the leader first. And by definition, the leader doesn't know where the opportunities are because they're just joining. And a lot of times, they are trying to do stuff that the startup isn't ready for. Whereas, if you're building it internally, like validating that you've had these big opportunities and you've already had some big wins, then bringing in the leader, you are usually more ripe to have long-term success there.

The Marketing Team at This Stage

The question we get most often at this stage is, do I need a CMO?

We will go out on a limb here and say that you likely do *not* need a CMO at this stage. You may be the exception, and you may have a good reason for making that hire, but typically you aren't ready to invest at this level just yet.

What is more important is what you should be looking for. You certainly need a point person who can manage this whole process. In your role as founder and leader, it is probably not the best use of your time to get in and manage all the variables of the testing process. It is too in the weeds for the founder to think about all the moving parts of the marketing program.

You do need certain resources at this stage. Depending on a variety of factors, you may make decisions to hire a staff, or you may use consultants. You may lean on an agency for help or contract support. However to get the job done, you will need some resources to help you move to the next stage of growth.

Folia Grace, VP of Marketing of TalkDesk, on Timing

Timing is a big issue. On one hand, I see organizations try to spend money too quickly, to invest in too much marketing too quickly, but they really haven't got the product and the ideal customer profile defined. There is just this idea that they can just go out and sell and market and that they're going to see this flood of business. And then they spend a lot of money and don't get results. So that's on the one side that overspending too early.

And then on the flip side, I see the startups that take the approach of having a proven model and a substantial number of customers. They want to do some more marketing and want to keep revenues coming in, but they want to be more profitable so they decide to not spend too much.

However, you can't build a roaring fire with kindling.

Now they think about bringing in a VP or a CMO to run marketing for them. They might have had a person running demand generation for them, but they realize they need someone more strategic—they need press or analyst relations, or they need work on their brand, things that might not have been priorities before then.

So now they are looking for a head of marketing or CMO. But there tends to be some confusion or debate about what type of person to bring in. You have pent-up demand from your sales team or for revenue, so they want leads or revenue. But then you need a product marketing background because you have to have the right messaging and the right strategy to find the right market with the right buyers. But everyone wants someone who has done it all, who is good at all of it. But I think the answer has to do with your company and what strategy you have, how well you know your buyer, and how confident you are in your message.

Head of Marketing Role

If you don't have one already, you probably need a head of marketing. You need one person who serves as the point person to help you execute your testing and develop a playbook going forward. This person could be an external party, but you are going to want someone who can see the bigger picture, understands the strategy, develops a plan to test all the moving pieces, analyzes them, and then develops the playbook. This person needs not only run and manage that process but also to be able to execute—with some help—all of the different messages and channels and variables in that campaign.

This person is going to be the leadership representative for this line of business, for this discipline in the organization. They can be a CMO in training or a junior CMO. But their focus should be to help pull all the pieces together from external and internal resources and to help the organization execute. They should be able to interact with other leaders in the organization and help make decisions with their internal partners.

You ideally want a marketing leader who has some experience they can directly leverage toward your go-to-market strategy. However, at this stage, your go-to-market approach may still change drastically. So the more important criteria for your head of marketing are their creativity, flexibility, test-and-learn attitude, and ability to lead the team and communicate with the rest of the organization.

Why Not a CMO?

This person may become the CMO, but rarely do people evolve through all of these stages of marketing growth. The head of marketing has to see the big picture, but they are more execution oriented—call it strategic execution—instead of the CMO you will need down the road. That CMO will develop strategy, develop leaders, develop campaigns and programs, manage the business and budgets, partner with leaders across the organization, and be the ambassador of the brand. That is a tall order and will require some investment in time and money to find the right person. If you get that person too early in the process (at this stage, for instance), you have taken that big role and expected them to execute with a small staff and focus on the tactical details. Many CMOs will be challenged at the level of detail-oriented execution.

Similarly, this head of marketing may not scale to the next role. If they are detail oriented, they may not have the requisite skills to manage and lead the entire business. It doesn't mean that they can't or won't grow into it, but they may not scale. Investing in the wrong level of resource results in unnecessary churn and a significant loss of time and money for that resource.

What you will have at the end of this stage is an understanding of the type of CMO you need to help you scale and grow the business. You may need a dynamic leader who inspires employees and customers alike, or an operational leader who can focus on running the business, or a data-driven leader who can get into the details of what helps a customer buy. These are all very different types of CMOs, and waiting until you have clarity may help you avoid unnecessary costly mistakes.

Bryan Kramer, author and TED speaker, thinks of hiring like naming a child:

> Culture is what make the brand unique. And you can't make that part up. It's like naming a child. And then the child becomes a personality, and that personality actually drives back to the name, and you start to associate that name more with the personality of the child than anything else. Same thing for culture; you can't really predict it, but you must you hire on brand, and eventually then it gets dictated by the culture and the tone of that culture, and then people start to make that culture even stronger—or not. And if you see a culture not being stronger it's because either you hired the wrong people or you have the wrong brand. You haven't identified exactly who your brand is. So it really is one of the most challenging jobs out there, because you're trying to set your whole company up for success.

Marketing Analysis Role

You probably don't need a data scientist—for these campaigns, anyway. And you probably won't have a person called head of data. But you do need an analytical skill set at this stage. You do need someone who is focused on measuring your programs and able to analyze and understand the results. As we discussed before, you will want to build your measurements into your programs, and this person will be key to helping you do that.

What many organizations do is get a growth marketer to do this. What this means is that the person running your campaigns is data driven and has some understanding of how to measure success. Again, this person may be separate from the person running your campaigns, but this focus on data is key.

An Iterative/Experimental Skill Set

One of the other skill sets you are hiring for is someone who is experimental. Just like any discipline, some marketers play into their comfort zone, while others want to branch out and try new things. You very much want the latter at this stage. You are going to be asking this person to explore new channels and messages and ways to deliver that to your customer, to help you find your customer and target them. This requires someone who is great dealing in ambiguity. This team may try 10 programs and nine may fail—not just fail, but fail miserably. They need to be okay with that, because they know one of them will eventually lead them to the successful solution. Not everyone is comfortable with being "right" only 10% of the time.

Kate Bradley Chernis

I believe that there's only three things that any marketer really needs; this is super simple and it hasn't changed since the dawn of time. Those three things are really good writing, really solid organizational skills, and then chutzpah. I can't do much about the chutzpah; that's in your court!

This type of mindset is crucial at this stage; however, it may be detrimental at later stages. A person prone to experimentation and always looking for a new path, a new way to do things, works great at this stage. But when you get to the next stage, which is about scaling programs and executing just one or two programs, they may find that rigor disquieting. Some people like to go from zero to 80 miles per hour; others like to take it from 80 to 81—big, bold moves versus rigorous iteration.

Channel-Specific Expertise

As you develop your playbook, you will begin to feel a greater need for more specific expertise, be it in PR, paid advertising, social media, analyst relations, or another area. With most of these specific roles, until you are ready to make a bet on an approach, it is best to look for help with existing team members or to get temporary help from external resources to help you with the execution. Put another way: why ramp up a PR person or team only to find out that you don't need press and media support. Or a search engine optimization (SEO) leader who is sitting on their hands 80% of the time after their initial work.

The trade-off that happens in many organizations is the blend of existing staff—who may be able to do "good enough" work—against bringing in subject matter experts to can help on specific, targeted execution of your programs. A good rule of thumb here is to never invest in something you can't easily "return" until you are sure it is the best investment for you and fits to your long-term strategy. If you aren't sure or if you still need to test and evolve, it's best to rent resources until you are sure. From single-shingle consultants to agencies or using online marketplaces for resources (our illustrator was found using 99designs.com), finding fractional or temporary talent may be the better way to go, especially while you are experimenting.

Marketing Technology Investments

At this stage you will start to make some investment in your infrastructure and your MarTech stack—your technology. As you start to make these investments, even for the basic foundation (your website or marketing automation tools), one thing to consider is ROI (return on investment).

As you have grown and built your marketing thus far, you have had more direct connection between investment and revenue. At this stage, you will be making some infrastructure investment that won't have direct impact on revenue.

This idea of delayed gratification can be challenging for organizations that are still proving their go-to-market strategy and their revenue model. Remember, at this stage you haven't proven the secret sauce for revenue, so the idea of spending on infrastructure at this stage can be awkward.

While the next phase may require significant investment in your marketing infrastructure, this phase should require just the basics to allow you to be malleable and flexible as you still figure out your playbook.

Courtney Kramer, CMO for CTI, put it this way:

> I would say the number one thing is to plan. You'd be surprised how many people are shocked that they need a plan, because they just think it's time to go straight to creative, and then on to implementation, and that is not the case.
>
> I mean actually putting it together in a physical plan, so as much as it sounds like it might be a waste of time even for a small team. Put your ideas and your thought processes down in even a PowerPoint: Here is our strategy and how we're going to approach it here. Here are some of the tactics that are going to hang off of that. And here are measurable goals that we want to get out of that experience is just super important. But these all helped us decide where we wanted to go as an organization together, what are our goals for this next year, and how do we use that to plan together.

The variables for your investment will vary, and we could write an entire book on all the moving pieces. There are approximately 6,800 distinct MarTech solutions available to help you reach your customer. This does not include the countless business tools and platforms you can utilize or the combinations of these that will help you find success. The sheer numbers are daunting. Therefore, it is best to wait before making any significant or long-term investment in these tools or solutions. There are a wealth of subscription service solutions that will allow you the flexibility to get a best-in-class product that can be scaled as needed.

Anand Thaker on Technology Recommendations

Get on social media, be active, listen to what's going on. You will get a lot of good advice and a lot of bad advice from it. If you're already doing your homework, you're already engaged in the space, you're probably figuring out who really knows what they're talking about, who really knows what's going on in the space, and what kind of recommendations they have been making. You could, hopefully you'll get some advice from that as a result of it.

The next best source is going to be the people around you. If you have a mentor or you have an advisor or maybe you already have a consultant in some sort of way, that's probably another good source of finding what you need to do next, or what you need to bring in house as a result of that in terms of technology. If you don't already have someone like that, ask them if they know other people. If you trust them, you believe in them, then that's a great way of doing it.

If you don't have that at your disposal, go back out to the social network, start asking. You will get every vendor under the sun talking about how great their solution is in some creative way, but listen to the people that are the closest to you or the people that have shown success that aren't trying to sell you something. That's usually very beneficial.

One misstep we have seen organizations make at this stage is to skip the testing phase and invest heavily in infrastructure. The problem is that they are then committed to a solution or platform of tools that may no longer meet their needs as their business evolves. There are a lot of great tools and technologies out there, and they keep growing, updating, and evolving. You may be getting swayed to make big bets on one or a few of these and commit your limited resources and budget to these. Be cautious. As marketers, we love our bright and shiny new tools, and many of these could make the campaign we are testing work better or be quicker or seem to cost less. However, if your marketer is not looking at the longer-term strategy and realizing that this is a time for testing and experimenting, they may opt for a solution that is not in the best interest of the business in the longer term. Make sure you know your requirements and that your chosen applications will work together.

Recent data showed that 89% of professional marketers are lacking in the technical skills to run the MarTech stack.

Plan to spend some money on tools, but try to avoid any long-term commitments as you test.

Moving Forward

We know at this point the clock is ticking and you're antsy to just get going already. But this is just like pausing to design your product before you build it. By taking some time to test your options and plan your next steps, you're more likely to see a return on your marketing dollars and scale more successfully.

Unfortunately, there is no exact aha moment that tells you that you have completed this stage. If you have a playbook of messaging and programs that work to reach customers, if you have the basis for your MarTech stack and know what it will take to grow it, and if you have the right talent to both manage your needs today and grow for your future, you are likely ready to combine them into a marketing plan that shifts these programs into high gear to grow your business.

6

GROW THE BUSINESS

The looming question at this stage:

- I'm ready to turn up my marketing investment; what do I need to do?

This chapter will cover:

- Developing a marketing plan
- Building out your marketing team, including hiring a marketing leader
- Managing the customer relationship throughout their entire journey
- Technology investments to support marketing programs
- Identifying new directions for growth

Todd had one especially memorable experience with a founder at this stage. This is one of those lessons that you appreciate only later in life. He was relatively junior in his career but was tasked with marketing the company for explosive growth. Some steps had been skipped along the way, and the process was not as evolved as described in this book, but nevertheless, the company was growing rapidly. A path had been set, and budgets were established—full speed ahead. Years later, Todd would reflect on what he should have done better and how what happened may have been better addressed, but tension with the founder started to escalate quickly. He had always played a hands-on role with product and product development but had never had a marketing team that was this active and "out there" in the market. Up to this point, marketing's role was limited to changes to the website and managing events.

The tensions came from the concepts of "quick" and "hands-on." Again, Todd would learn how to effectively work across those philosophies later in his career. But for this circumstance, the company was not ready for rapid growth. The leadership was not prepared for the speed it would require to grow that quickly. The processes were not in place to make decisions at scale at the velocity the business was moving. The founder and marketing were butting heads.

This is going to be a phase of trust. This can be a challenging time for founders. Up until this stage, the founder has been more deeply involved in marketing. This stage will test the founder's ability to step back and let marketing run their business. This means bringing in a VP or CMO to help drive this forward. This means investing in marketing infrastructure and trusting that those investments will pay off. This will mean that the time testing and iterating will pay off as you invest in marketing programs that drive growth.

The wait is over. At this phase, you are ready to step on the gas and grow the business. In the prior phases, you defined your product or service, you found a fit in the marketplace, you tested your approach to reach your customer, and now you are ready to drive explosive growth in the market. How you define that may vary—for some it may be about running after 15 large, targeted accounts, while for others it may be going after millions of consumers. Whatever your aspirations, this phase is about making it happen.

This is about creating an execution engine. This is about scale. This is all about repeatability. Here we dial back the experimentation and focus on discipline. It's time to turn that playbook into a marketing plan and execute. This is a time for investment and a rotation toward a focus in your marketing of the business.

Focus of This Stage

This stage means some pretty heady investment in programs, technology, and talent. It also means focusing on the customer. Up to this point, most organizations have focused on the next immediate goal—building a product, finding a fit, finding prospects, winning customers, and so on. Now is the time to start thinking about what happens *after* your next goal: What happens after you win your customer? What do you want that relationship to look like? For many founders, the focus has been on the idea, that thing that is unique to your organization and to your market. At this stage, that dream of your big idea being used by a marketplace can now come true, but you have to determine what you want from this relationship with your customer.

It is time to turn that relationship into a commitment and pivot your focus toward keeping and strengthening it. This is the stage where you invest in your customers, win them over, make good on your promise to them, and build a long-term relationship with them.

One thing that founder Jason Saffron built upon is the lessons from his father, who was a salesperson for home furnishings. His dad would watch his sales teams walk someone around the floor and show them every lamp in the place and then say, "Hope to see you soon," as the person was leaving the store. His dad instilled in him this idea of "never be afraid to ask for what you want." So many people—business leaders included—get to this stage and then never work to get the customer to buy, never to close. From Jason's perspective, the worst they are going to say is no. But this fear to not go after what you want (which is to get people to buy and use your product) sets in, and this fear is toxic.

The Customer Journey

On the face of it, this may sound like buzzy (or cringeworthy) jargon your marketing teams like to throw around. But this is time to start looking at the all the places you interact with the customer—from that first time they notice you all the way through their experiences after they become a customer. Most businesspeople are familiar with the idea of the funnel as the path that customers move through until they reach the end and become a customer.

The modern version of the funnel is more a circular route, where the customer moves through the decision to purchase your product and then they become a customer. For subscription businesses or any businesses with potential repeat purchases, continuing to invest in these relationships can make or break your company. Acquiring a new customer is anywhere from five to 25 times[10] more expensive than retaining an existing one, depending on your industry (and which study you believe). If you spend money to acquire customers only to lose them later in the cycle, those are wasted dollars. So it is important to find and fix any leaks. Even more so, those customers, if happy, can become advocates for your organization, telling others through word of mouth or leaving reviews, or helping to bring new customers to you to help you grow your business organically.

Bill Macaitis has this to say about customer recommendations:

> Marketing's role is to help spread the word, to increase that growth, to give prospects and customers an amazing experience, and ultimately, I think the bar is to get people to recommend you, not just to get people to buy from you. When I worked at Slack, that's what I told my team members: "We're not in the business of just getting people to buy our product. We're in the business of getting people to recommend us because all the fundamentals, all your cash payback, your magic number, everything just works better when you've got a really strong healthy growth rate that comes from organic word of mouth."

You and your leadership team, including marketing, should plan on thinking about the entire journey you are taking the customer on with you. You may have specific challenges that you need to resolve in specific parts of this journey—like creating awareness—but you should look at the journey holistically to ensure a consistent and great experience. This analysis can help you identify the major gaps and priority investments you need to make.

10   Amy Gallo, "The Value of Keeping the Right Customers," Harvard Business Review online, October 29, 2014, https://hbr.org/2014/10/the-value-of-keeping-the-right-customers.

Every marketer has their own ideas of what each stage of this journey is called. But in general, they fall into five simple categories, which organizations like McKinsey and other consultancies have been advocating for years:

- Awareness
- Familiarity
- Consideration
- Purchase
- Loyalty

- **Awareness:** This is that first interaction you have with the customer. It can be as simple as them seeing your name for recognition later or a deeper understanding, but the customer has "woken up" to you, even if they don't fully understand who you are just yet. We are pummeled with these messages daily. For most of us this is just white noise in the market. Does that pharmaceutical company really think I am going to remember the name Xhimalta? No, but if you hear it 10–20 times and then your doctor mentions it as a possibility for you, you have that "Oh, wait, I've heard of that" moment.

- **Familiarity:** This stage means they now have some sense of who you are and what you do. You are a possibility for them, even if it's down the road. But they have a general sense of you and what you can do. You make an impulse buy to move this quickly to the next stage, or you may store this information for a late purchasing decision. But you have a sense of the basic features and what benefit they may be to you.

- **Consideration:** This stage is a determination of your product or service as it relates to the customer. They have gone from passive understanding to an active stage of making a decision. This is a great stage for your product marketing organization. It is connecting the buyers needs to the specifics of the product or service. It is about helping that buyer realize the value the product creates and helping them overcome any barriers to making that decision (price, convenience, etc.).

- **Purchase:** This is the active stage of making a purchase of your product or service. This can be instantaneous or for complex sales may take months to actually secure. This is about getting the buyer to move across their Rubicon, their point of no return.

- **Loyalty:** This stage is a major reason we typically move away from the funnel discussion. Loyalty is both how they are treated and how they perceive you post sale. What are they doing to do for or against you as your relationship continues. One important point about loyalty: we have seen many organizations fail at this stage because they view the sale as the end, or they see loyalty as the challenge of the customer success or the service and support organization. However, your customer has a voice and several platforms on which they can share their perspectives on you and your organization. Even if they never (have to) buy another thing from you ever again, are they going to persuade others to buy or steer clear of you?

As your organization enters this stage of your business, you may have a few successful customer relationships, and you may have a great idea of how to manage those relationships. Your marketing organization is critical to helping to establish a great connection between you and your customer. You may be focused on just one specific stage or may be targeting your customer across multiple stages. It is important to see how these all fit together. If you are running programs to help them with purchasing decisions, but they have no awareness of you, you are missing your customer. If you are spending a great deal of time and energy on creating awareness, but you have a disloyal group of customers who are trashing you publicly, your organization will appear tone deaf, and that energy spent to get customers to notice you will have the exact opposite result—they will notice you and have a negative perception of you. In that scenario, it would have been better to not have them notice you at all.

You can think about your approach as different horizons. Horizon 1 is the short-term things you need to do, things in the next six months. Horizon 2, you start thinking for your business and how you plan the next six to 18 months. Horizon 3 are things you're planning for that will impact your business in 12 to 24 months. Some businesses can only deal with the next six months. They can only think through this whole concept of horizon 1. It's just all they have time for. Whenever possible, plan for these horizons using the same timetables that are used by your customers. This will further help you line up to their decision cycles and get you into the discipline of how they think about their businesses.

Once you're in a place where you can start thinking more long term around your business, about product roadmap, and about where your company is going, and you have a degree of stability, that's when this whole idea of customer lifetime value starts to click and make sense. I've seen more and more business, especially SaaS businesses that are starting to switch to horizon 2 a lot earlier and starting to ask key questions about customer lifetime value, from "How do I drive this sort of immediate revenue growth" to "How do I think a little bit more holistically? How do I think more about product adoption, and how do I think more about experience in driving value for customers?"

Bill Macaitis

At Slack, we intentionally organized the sales, marketing, success, and support teams together because those were all the primary customer-facing teams. Those teams had a lot of interactions with prospects and customers on a daily basis, and we felt uniting them under one banner or one leader would allow us to look at that journey more holistically and think about what those handoffs are and how can we provide a delightful experience, a better experience. We would talk about codifying our editorial tone and values, and we wanted to speak in a very human tone and a relatable tone. We would never use acronyms.

There is a little bit of fun, too, a little bit of whimsy, and once we codified that we then trained all the customer-facing teams: our sales team, our marketing team, our success team, our support team. Were we sticking to our core values as a company? Were they writing in the style and tone that we just described? So I think that's a good example of something where you say you want to be customer-centric and put yourselves in their shoes and move that from an organizational structure from a process structure. I think another thing that really drives it is the metrics you use.

So if you say you're customer-centric, what metrics are you using to incentivize your teams? People are good because they want to do well, and if they're told, "Hey, this is your primary metric," they're going to do whatever they can. Historically we talk about marketing being judged solely based on leads, and leads can be slanted. You can find ways to get spikes and leads that are really bad experiences for the customer.

You know a lot of the metrics we've classically used for these go-to-market teams are usually judged on how little they spend. Success is judged on how much more they sold, sales is judged based on how big of a deal they got—marketing and leads and all of these things can incentivize very short-

term and non-good, non-friendly customer-centric behavior. Sales can tend to oversell, overpromise. You know, maybe put them on plans they don't need or put more people on it.

To be customer-centric, leadership has to embrace it. I'm a huge believer that putting on the customer-centric path is the strongest way to achieve hypergrowth and to achieve long-term differentiation in the space.

Customer Journey Mapping

Explicitly mapping out the details of a typical customer's journey with your company and understanding where you have the most issues and where you are losing customers or prospects will help clarify and align your leadership to focus on the right priorities to grow your business. There is no sense in spending a lot of money to generate leads if sales isn't following up with the leads to turn them into opportunities and close deals. And why pay sales to close deals if there are major product onboarding issues and customers give up before they even get to discover the value of the product? Map out the customer's entire path from the point they learn about you as far as you can (including renewal or expansion). Figure out where the biggest holes are, and plug them first.

Bill Macaitis on Brand as a Differentiator

I've always believed in a brand having a personality. It is such an easy differentiator from your competition. The color scheme, the visual identity, the editorial tone and voice—that's not something that you need to spend $10 million to do. Any company of any size can kind of go through that exercise and just talk about how you want to be unique, how you want to be different.

I work with a lot of companies on the advising side and the board side. I was going through the website and the brand with one, and it was sterile lifeless black and white. I mean I was falling asleep even reading about it, and it looked like every other competitor in their space. And I think there's this prevailing view that if you're in B2B you have to be serious and monotone and use acronyms and say you're a disrupting platform...

And every single screen on a white background or always using black text. And they had cheesy stock photo shots of people sitting around a conference room, and I just thought, that is such an incredible missed opportunity to differentiate yourself.

I love the brands that you have a relationship with and you root for and you recommend. And I think going through that process of saying, hey, how can we differentiate even from a color scheme perspective. If you look at Slack, it could have been black and white but wow, it shows a very bold tartan plaid color scheme, that's very differentiated.

The editorial tone and voice, when Slack loads it takes a little while to load on the desktop. It could have been a little hourglasses there but instead it shows a fun inspirational message of the day, right. We put that in there to make people smile. And if you've seen the Slack TV and YouTube ads, you know there's a lot of personality to them and there's a lot of emotion. And you laugh and you smile and it's not a standard transactional, sign up today, free trial 20% off. It's about the emotion that you feel.

Marketing Plan

This stage begins with the creation of a marketing plan that combines the playbook you developed and your customer journey work. This doesn't have to be incredibly complex but should clearly communicate to all stakeholders what marketing is doing so you can ensure alignment and assess any potential new investments against it. The marketing plan should include:

- Goals: What are you trying to achieve?
- Metrics: How you will measure success?
- Strategy: High-level approach to achieving those goals.
- Plan: Programs you plan to run, with goals.
- Budget: How much do you plan to spend?
- Additional testing and experimentation budget.

In a startup, your marketing plan will likely change and evolve often, as you learn. You may need to draft a plan at the start of the year, but expect it to change. It is best to update your plan quarterly or at least every half year.

Investment Strategy

As you build your marketing engine to run these programs at scale, your investments will have to align across programs, technology, and people. You know who you want to address in the market and you know how to find them, but your investment needs to be smart across all three of these levers.

Each of these investments must blend with the others. Overloading in one area will diminish your overall results. Having an amazing CMO without a program budget or resources is frustrating for all parties involved. Building the best tech stack with no one to adequately run it is equally as bad.

The biggest issue for many founders at this stage is trust. Your organization is now going to shift resources from one area of the business to another. This is new for many founders, and while it may sound straightforward on paper, it is a challenge for many companies. Previously, investments in product have yielded enhancements in that product. The return has been calculated and felt by the organization. Now that part of the business will receive less funding and marketing will ramp up. But there is going to be a gap where trust becomes an issue. You are making critical investments in your organization, and those investments take time to yield fruit. Getting this engine moving—even when you know exactly what you want to do—also takes time. Also, customers are not trained dogs; they don't just come when you call them. All of this will take some time to execute and see results; meanwhile, the immediacy of some of the underfunded organization will be felt immediately. This is uncomfortable for even the most seasoned executives.

Manish Gupta, CMO at Redis Labs, has this to say about trust:

> What happens is in the earliest stages of the company is that in a smaller setting you invest in an area and you are able to see the results in a pretty quick manner. That behavior and that expectation becomes sort of set in the culture of the startup environment. When you get to a scaled environment or as you plan for a hyperscale and hypergrowth mode, you may have to invest ahead of the curve, and the results from that investment and that foundation may not be obvious in a short duration.

So it requires a little bit of leap of faith from the founding team and from the rest of the management team and the investment team to be able to support the new executive or the CMO initiatives, to say these are necessary to not only go to a 50,000,000 but perhaps when we go to 100,000,000, if you don't have these things in place, you may actually break the model at some point. That can be a challenge, and I've noticed when that is actually executed, too, it works well, and when that becomes a bit of a difficult decision to handle because the visibility may take longer, then that can be difficult and impediment to success and acceleration of growth.

There is an opportunity for a different kind of investment at this stage of your company's growth—an investment in leadership. As you and your marketing team are building and running this infrastructure, it will require your marketing leadership to partner with the heads of finance, technology, and talent as you require money, tech, and people to run marketing. Teams often become siloed and play their role in the organization. As a CEO, as a leader, opportunities to get teams to truly interact, roll up their sleeves, and work together can be rare and should not be wasted. This is a great opportunity for your marketing leadership to find coconspirators across the organization and work to build a well-run, modern marketing organization, supported by finance, technology, and HR.

Margaret Molloy on the Role of the CMO
The channels have evolved, the pace of change has changed, and the need to be strategic and understand the market remains constant. The role of the CMO in my view is to have a strategic outlook and appreciate the duality of creativity and analysis in the marketing process. It seems to me that great CMOs need to be able to take in many data inputs, they need to have an appetite for change, to be able to synthesize insights, articulate brand purpose that is compelling for their colleagues and others. And at its heart, that's about understanding a lot of inputs and being able to simplify them for an audience. So great CMOs in my mind are great simplifiers.

Invest in Programs

You have tested and iterated in your prior steps. The pilots have proven to be successful. Now is the time to invest heavily in these programs. The payoff for running those pilots can be felt now. If you have run those iterative tests to determine which programs work best, you can easily build an ROI model here. Your budget can be determined by the success of your pilots. Put another way, you should have a pretty good sense that $1 of program spend will yield you a specific result. The result may be qualified leads, or website traffic, or actual revenue. But it should be a straightforward exercise to build your budgets off of this ROI model.

It will never be perfect, and there are too many variables to say that this is concrete, established math. Even if you feel you "know" exactly what this model looks like, it will still change on you over time. Testing never fully ends. However, this idea of ROI for your programs changes the conversation for marketing and for leadership.

Typically marketing has been the land of the ask and the land of the spend. One CFO opined that marketing was the place where money was never enough and the appetite was never satiated. That may be true, but building off of piloted programs and then developing the ROI model is a great way for marketing and finance to collaborate and drive the business.

The ROI model also allows marketing to truly be the stewards of revenue for the organization. Whether you have a sales organization or a digital point-of-sale model, the marketing organization can own and manage the revenue stream for the organization.

Up to now, you will have seen a more direct connection between investment and revenue. As one CEO put it to us, "I will gladly give you $60,000 if you can show me how this is going to bring in $1M in revenue." That direct connection—or often close to direct connection—helps you responsibly manage your business and your limited resources to invest in your growth. This is also why time was invested in to the prior phase of testing to help avoid costly mistakes and expenses in areas that failed to yield return.

At this stage of investment, it will become more challenging in certain infrastructure expenses to make that direct connection to return on your invest-ment. In fact, for many of these investments, ROI goes out the window. They become a cost of doing business. While this may be more comfortable and more obvious for, say, the costs of desks or phones or internet for your employees, this may be the first time you have invested in marketing without direct return.

What is of critical importance for this role is that marketing can both recognize the success of these programs and communicate the status to the organization. Building metrics into your programs and having the people or technology to analyze and communicate those metrics is the responsibility of marketing team and comes with the trust that the leadership has placed in marketing to be the stewards of revenue.

One common mistake for analysis and reporting is that people often develop the plan first, then ask, "How are we going to measure it?" This makes reporting a "snap-on" step at the end of your program, and it seldom works. Measuring should actually be the first step—the very first question—in developing and running these programs: "What does success look like? What do we want to accomplish? How do we know when we have that—how do we measure it?"

Start with a goal-oriented approach and determine what you have in place—or will need to have in place—to measure the success of your program. This may sound intuitive, but not having it is uncomfortably common. Great programs are developed, and then a "square peg, round hole" approach is forced to measure. For instance, if you are going to run an event-based strategy, how will you measure success? Is it the number of business cards collected? What if people don't carry cards? Is it badge scans? Do you know that the person you want to talk to is at that event? Is your success just about the leads? If not, what are going to do to measure the other goals?

Most often this applies to digital marketing plans. One recent company wanted to run ads on Facebook. Now, there are great analytics for Facebook ads, but the goal was amorphous. "Let's drive leads" was the rallying cry. But an ad alone won't do that. As the program was developed, knowing what you wanted to see happen at each stage needed to be measured. How many times does the prospect see the ad? When do they click it? How much time do they spend on site? When do we lose them? How often do they take the next steps? What happens when given a lead form?

Marketing and leadership should have a sense that this whole process is being managed and run effectively, that these questions are being asked, and that the tools to answer them are put in place.

There are circumstances in which you can't answer these questions, or you have to use secondary—more intuitive—measures to answer them. Just because something happens online, for instance, doesn't mean you can track and measure everything. There are times when you have to make assumptions, but it is important for the team to agree on those assumptions and what they believe they mean. You may make a major press release. It will be challenging to prove that the announcement—especially if that announcement is picked up and broadcast across a few media outlets or sites—caused some behavior in your consumer. However, if you see a spike in web traffic or a spike in people visiting that product page for 72 hours after the release and there wasn't another coinciding event, you can probably assume this was related to the release.

This may sound intuitive and even simple, but it is a constant source of frustration for founders and leaders who believe that every step is measurable or that marketing is not holding up their end of the bargain by being able to measure the steps of this process. This is why having agreement on what is measurable, what is assumed, and what is neither can be so important to reinforcing the trust between the marketing team and the rest of the organization.

Invest in Technology

A critical part of your spending mix will go to technology. In 2011 there were about 150 MarTech companies to help you run your marketing organization. They were more than eager to help you spend your money with them. Many of these companies are household names for marketers and leaders and are part of your de facto tech stack. However, over the years, more and more companies have become part of this landscape. As of the time of publication, there are 6,800 companies in this space—that is only for the MarTech space and does not include the myriad of scheduling, automation, or productivity technologies to support your teams. The vastness of opportunities to invest in is why technology follows programs in order of your spend. It is incredibly easy to be sold on great tech—and then try to find a place to use it in your organization. The creativity and inventiveness of the tools in this space is truly impressive. But before you start laying down the corporate credit card to subscribe to these products, knowing your programs and how you are going to measure them will save you both money and migraines.

Anand Thaker offers this critical piece of advice:

> Technology only magnifies the people, processes, and data behind them. If you're doing really well and you're very authentic—you are handling things really well on paper or Excel or everyday technologies—if you're doing it well, then technology will help magnify that. If you're doing things poorly from the beginning, guess what? Technology is not going to navigate that for you.

Even the best practices don't say, "Go use this technology in this way." It says, "Do these five steps or adopt this mindset," and then that is how the technology will support you. The good technology vendors want you to be good at what you're doing before you start implementing their technology. It is in their best interest to make you successful and to keep you using them for a long time, so they want to help you. They want to make sure the technology is enabling you in the right way.

Have a plan and stick to it. These technologies are really great shiny toys. There are great ways to streamline and automate your programs and processes. They are also a great way to spend money and not fully understand the costs—resources to implement or align processes. Even great SaaS technology that offers "seamless integration" always requires something to align to their technology. It is people or processes or some other technology. The "cost" may be minimal, but know that it is there.

On the other side, there is a necessary frugality for organizations at this stage. Teams can underinvest in technology with the thought "We can just do that ourselves." It is important that the resource costs are considered for your spend. Technology will be your best friend, but not all of your best friends are there for a lifetime.

Your technology spend can fall into two main categories: program spend and infrastructure spend. Your program spend is what you need to run your programs and campaigns. Your infrastructure spend is what you need to run your business. It is the foundation of your marketing and supports your marketing team.

The reason for the distinction is how you categorize your spend. Your program technology spend should be part of your ROI calculation for your programs. Your infrastructure technology spend should be treated separately and budgeted as part of your investment in marketing. The infrastructure investment is necessary—think of this as your CRM system or the cost of servers to support the website—to run your business. Many teams still treat this all as one budget, which makes it infinitely more challenging to scale pieces up and down effectively as you see results of your programs. By separating out your infrastructure and program technology spend, you can establish a budget with finance to build your marketing organization, while you have a more fluid budget for programs that allows you to make smart decisions on which levers to pull to drive revenue.

As you and your marketing team looks to acquire your MarTech stack, this is a great opportunity to build collaboration and trust between marketing and your CTO (or whoever is running your technology). While many of these MarTech solutions are subscription and may not seem like challenging decisions to make, collaborating will allow your technology teams to help marketing make smarter decisions, recognize opportunities to utilize technology in other parts of the business and to, in some cases, bring licensing and implementation costs down.

Anand says this about how to start this process:

> There are really four main paths here. One, it doesn't hurt to have a consultant who's done this before come in and help you figure out what that stack needs to look like. Two, some of the major vendors have good partner programs. They could recommend partners to come and help you with that. That's not a bad way of going, especially if you've already made some significant investment with someone in a technology or services fashion.

Three is hiring somebody. If you're looking for the hire, you're probably at a point where you recognize you've got your processes in place, you're scaling very fast, and you're recognizing that the technology truly is limiting our ability to plug and play more people to go and help with that growth. Four, try this yourself. Try to figure out what technologies you need, and count on trusted advisors for counsel. No matter which way you go, when looking for people or guidance, one of the things you want to look for is some level of experience. They don't have to know everything. They don't have to know all 6,000 companies in the MarTech stack (there are only maybe two people in the world that have that kind of wisdom and information and intuition). You definitely want to see good problem solvers, people who like to play and who have demonstrated some level of success, and then ask them about their failures. Where did they screw up, and what lessons did they learn?

The leadership team can help broker this relationship and allow both marketing and technology to bring their subject matter expertise to the MarTech stack to help your company grow and expand. Everyone is moving quickly, and many of these decisions do not require a lengthy review process, but even simple collaboration goes a long way.

A critical investment for your team is in your analytics and reporting technology. Your programs will require tools to accurately report on your program effectiveness. While there are too many variables in determining the best mix for your organization, if there is one area to overinvest in, it may well be in analytics and reporting. So much of your success will be determined by the data to help you make smarter decisions going forward. You may invest in a really great ad, and it may look amazing, but if you don't know if that ad performed well or if you can't understand how to improve it, then you are lacking the correct tools to effectively run ads.

Analytics and reporting has been a hot growth space for well over two decades now. For as long as there has been a need to run marketing, there has been a need to know how well it is working. The improvements in technology are mind-blowingly fast. Machine learning and AI have accelerated leapfrog improvements. This also means investing time, energy, and resources into determining which are the best solutions for you now, and revisiting your decision over time as new technologies emerge. Whether you employ a data scientist or a smart technologist or Ted the summer intern to own this, it is important to have an owner in the organization and to support their learning in the space of the constant improvements. What is not easily measurable today may be seamless and effortless tomorrow.

Mike Moran on Taking Time to Build
You can't just from go from zero to 100, so this does need to be a series of steps. Start by focusing on the next right thing and build from there. What happens all too often is this desire to be perfect and accurate on day one. When that doesn't happen, leaders feel like the data doesn't work, and so they go back to their gut.

By focusing on the bigger-picture goals and then taking the necessary steps to get there, organizations can successfully build a data-driven culture. But no one is going to have perfect data on the first day, so setting those realistic expectations is critical.

You'll need the right technology to run your marketing programs. Along with that, you must have agreed on key performance indicators for your programs that are measurable, and you must have the right technology in place to measure them.

As you will see in the next section, having people to run your technology will be a critical component to determine if your technology actually runs.

Invest in People
The remaining piece of the marketing puzzle is people. As of the date publication, robots have not taken over the marketing function of your organization, and so you need great people to run your programs and allow your technology to support your growth. This includes a great leader. Now may be a perfect time to look for that perfect CMO.

Manish Gupta says this about hiring the right CMO:

> There are several things [to look for in a CMO], but the very first element is a recognition on both sides from the founder and team, and the CMO that this is a marriage that requires adjustment and appreciation on both fronts. So while the CMO might bring in the best of breed practices from the past experience, every culture in the company is unique, and those practices must melt in and work well within the culture, the environment, the rest of the team. So I think that appreciation of both sides, just like the founders have to trust a new set of practices that the CMO might bring to the other side as well.

Founder Dimitry Pavlov has this to say about bringing people into his organization:

> It is challenging for a founder to sit down and learn finance or operations or IT or marketing. It is a humbling experience—you built this company, and you're smart, but now you are putting yourself in a position where you don't know everything. This is where you need to trust yourself and look for mentors and people around you who can fill in the gaps, help you make smart decisions about who to hire and when.

Now that you have a sense of what programs to run and what your goals for growth are, you can find that perfect CMO for your organization. You may have a leader in place, and they may naturally fit that top job. Other times, you need that CMO DNA in your team and will start sourcing the marketing leader. This idea is explored more in chapter 8 on hiring and building. As you evaluate your current talent and look for this role, there are a few considerations.

Finding a CMO is as much about cultural fit as it is about talent. There are plenty of great, talented marketers out there. The marketing person is going to be the one in the marketplace talking about the product—they are the standard-bearer. This can be an uncomfortable place for many founders, as the product is their idea, their passion. Many have sacrificed and put much of themselves into the organization and into their product, their idea. Turning that over to a new person and asking them to help you promote this in the marketplace is daunting. So fit is crucially important here. Many organizations have failed with a miss in this critical relationship between founder and marketer. On paper, it should have worked, but that lack of trust never allowed the two leaders to collaborate and grow the company.

For many leaders, being able to identify marketers and understand their abilities is a challenge. Marketers—those who are exceptional at marketing—also know how to market and brand themselves. This is not an insinuation that they are being false or misleading but that for those who have not had strong relationships with marketing leadership, can be challenging to understand what a marketers core strengths are (and what they are not).

The leadership team should have clarity about the role the CMO will play over the next few years. This means not only running programs but building the MarTech stack, investing in people, and helping to analyze results to evolve the business over time. Just like the old adage "There is fast, cheap, and effective—pick two," you can't have everything, and this applies to the CMO. Understand which of programs, technology, people, and data/analysis is the most important and why. You don't have to settle for someone who is subpar in any of these. In fact, most candidates you will look at for CMO spots check all the boxes. But every marketer has come up the ranks through a particular marketing discipline, be it brand or product marketing or demand generation, and has a particular strength (and probably a corresponding weakness). A good CMO should be self-aware and able to hire and lead talent that complements their strength. They may be great at the hard skills, like programs and technology, but may lack in the soft skills, like people skills or cultural fit. Conversely, you may find a big, gregarious personality who is great onstage and wins over anyone in the room with them, but they may lack some technological sophistication. By this point you should be able to figure out your own strengths and weaknesses and the needs of your organizations to determine the kind of CMO you need to complement your skills and lead the organization where it needs to go.

For Erica Brescia, co-founder and COO of Bitnami, having a strong sense of who she needed in this role was key"

> I spent time talking to a mentor at Y-Combinator who gave me great advice. I don't think enough founders do that—go get great advice. She really helped me understand what kind of marketer we were looking for. We received over 100 resumes from some really great marketers. On one hand, we are honored that people wanted to come work with us, but finding that best CMO for us required us to be secure in the type of leader and the types of skill sets we were looking for.

As a leadership team, as you think across these evaluation points, understand who in the organization can support their weaker areas and where you can find some exponential benefit to their strengths. Where most organizations struggle with this decision is in building a job description just about the marketing programs you want to run, and then finding that the leader is exposed and failing in other key areas of the business. Remember, this CMO is not just the head of marketing but also a supporting leader in the organization that helps other leaders and teams grow the business. A great CMO will also help drive product insights, recruit great talent with HR, help finance communicate to key stakeholders, and so on. The CMO is not just a marketer, so look for talent that helps the role live beyond the marketing organization.

There will also be recommendations by the company's supporting network. Many CMOs have been brought in because of stellar relationship with board members or advisors. These introductions can be extremely valuable for the leadership team. However, no one knows better what is best for the organization than the leadership team. Prior success at another organization or a recommendation should be considered, but you, your team, and your organization are unique—in the truest meaning of the word—and therefore each CMO candidate should be judged on what you need for your unique situation.

There is also a general school of thought to wait to make any other critical hires until this CMO is in place. Each organization will have to come to their own conclusions as to how to approach this, but there are certain roles that you know you will need to help grow your business. As you think about speed, also consider longer-term goals for your organization. You may opt to wait on a few roles. Two roles you should consider bringing in regardless of your CMO decision are operations and analysis/reporting.

A good operations person can run the business as fluidly as it evolves. New technology, new processes, and new people can we woven into their responsibilities. But a solid operations person knows how to multitask and how to take on the additional responsibilities needed to help make the leader and the rest of the organization successful. Yes, finding a fit with the CMO is important and having an operations person who clashes with the CMO can be more than challenging. But waiting to find this critical person to help evolve and run the team can be just as damaging.

Your reporting and your ability to analyze the success of your programs will require a strong person to not only put this practice into operation, but to constantly question the data and the success of the program. A great person here intuitively looks under rocks to find answers and is not just building a report, but has an inquisitive nature to find answers.

It may be wise to wait for the CMO, but finding that perfect CMO may take months. Lacking in these two critical talent areas may be an undue burden for the organization. These two roles also are harder to find external or consultative talent to fill. There are great people who can do this for a shorter period of time, but both of these roles benefit from someone who can learn the business and is invested in the organizations success. Mining data for that nagging question or learning how to best utilize resources in the organization to bring about the desired results all takes time and energy to learn.

Ultimately, the CMO will be making decisions on how best to build these various pieces for the marketing organization. Establishing trust with that CMO will be crucial. The old saying "trust but verify" is a good litmus test here. The founder and the leadership team should not turn their back on the new market leader but support them and help them quickly make smart decisions for the business. No matter how smart and talented they are and how many times they have done this before, your organization is unique, and it will require time for them to learn it. The partnership between the leadership team and this new member will be key for everyone's success.

ABE

A LWAYS
B E
E VOLVING

The ABCs of sales are "always be closing." Any *Glengarry Glen Ross* fan will remember the iconic "always be closing" scene. This is true for the marketing organization as well, but even more important is ABE: always be evolving. Even as you invest in your programs, your technology, and your people, the process of testing and iterating and evolving never quite finished. What works for you today won't work tomorrow.

One company invested heavily in a field marketing strategy and one or two key seminal events. But as appetites changed, there were fewer and fewer decision makers at these shows. The number of attendees kept rising, but the decision makers stayed home. Without analyzing the results of their show strategy, the company might still be spending 50% of its budget on marketing to managers and assistants and miss talking to the VP-level decision makers.

A nimble team led by your CMO and supported by an inquisitive analyst and a flexible operations person can help your company quickly adapt to new trends and changing tastes. Your customer may change and grow more rapidly than you may like. New competition or threats may enter the market. Changes in the economy may change their willingness to think about your product. These data points need to be constantly read and adapted for.

It is important for a leadership team to support and encourage the CMO to keep investing time and energy in investigation. Often, the leader gets siloed into the role and is expected to solely perform, to execute. This should be the large focus of the role, but a good leader will set the tone that the path to revenue changes frequently and that the CMO should be focused on constantly finding the best ways to drive growth. This often means helping the organization not waste money by making bad decisions. The leadership team and the founder should look for the CMO to help educate the organization on what testing and evolution is happening—in concert with executing the strategy. Many CMOs will shy away from a conversation about failure. Testing falls off because the organization has established a strategy and their job is to then execute that strategy.

Encourage your CMO and marketing organization to continue to place small bets on testing new opportunities, to understand what is working and why, and to question why results are having diminishing returns. This may be put into practice as a percentage of time allowed to inquire and experiment, or it may simply be a philosophy of the organization, but failure to test will result in the inevitable scenario: a panic of diminishing results where costs rise or revenues fall—or both—and then radical moves to right the ship. These quick turns result in activity in search of a strategy. The marketing organization suddenly feels pressure to pivot, and the desire to execute precedes making the right decision.

Small micro adjustments along the way will help to forgo the inevitable panic scenario but require some practice and commitment up front. It is good practice to explicitly separate out a budget for testing and experimentation.

Casey Winters on Evolving the Marketing Organization
A practical tip to help with evolving the marketing organization: productivity is seldom high on Friday afternoons. Allow your teams to engage in four or five hours of inquisitive practice during the last few hours of the week. This will allow them to flex their creative muscles and will allow you to test and

iterate programs. This time can be used for exploring new technologies and demonstrations, having teams to tackle some problem in the organization, or testing and piloting a new program.

New Growth Directions (What Got You Here Won't Get You There)

At some point, when your business is on a good growth trajectory, you'll begin to consider additional directions where you can expand. You'll likely want to continue to find ways to further penetrate your current market. But the next obvious areas for expansion are:

1. Selling your existing product into new markets.
2. Developing additional products to sell into your existing market.

Each of these has its own challenges. You can't assume in either case that the market and growth will behave the same as your existing business, so it is generally best, particularly for new products, to treat these new businesses as exactly that and organize them as startups within your organization.

That means you may want to build a small team with its own budget and metrics and autonomy to test and iterate to figure out their path to market. If you burden them with the heavier processes and expectations of the more established business, you may be doomed to fail before you begin. For instance, the customer acquisition costs for new businesses will likely be higher early on before you have any awareness and as the team figures out the market and buyer journey. Given these challenges, trying to take on too many new directions at once will likely spread your team too thin and not give any the fuel they need for success.

Freshworks (originally Freshdesk) is known for building a cloud-based customer engagement product and business in India that competes successfully against entrenched incumbents like Zendesk and ServiceNow. They built out a low-touch, high-volume sales and marketing engine to drive that business. When their small business customer support product, called Freshdesk, was growing rapidly, the company added a second product, Freshservice, built off their initial product but aimed at IT departments. The company was smart in forming a small, focused team to launch the product and giving the team freedom to experiment to do what they needed to achieve product/market fit and grow. This approach made coordination and brand consistency more challenging but helped the new business succeed.

The market for this second product was really midmarket, which created some new challenges in selling. The team rapidly experimented and grew the second product even faster than the first. But it wasn't without challenges. Jill joined to help the company develop a US presence and expand upmarket. They added a US-based midmarket team to drive that expansion upmarket. But all of the company processes, structures, and messaging were designed around a frictionless self-service model for small businesses. And the core of the company, and the center of those processes, was across the world, in India. They eventually built a healthy growing business and expanded further to other regions. However, it took the new small team in California time and travel to India to build the relationships, expand the processes, and develop the messaging to enable midmarket sales and support.

If you're launching additional products, you'll also have to consider branding when you launch. Often startup companies names are synonymous with their first product. That name may or may not extend well to support your new lines of business, and you'll need to invest in driving awareness for all of your brands.

When Freshdesk launched its second product, they decided to extend the "Fresh" branding for this new product, naming it Freshservice. But customers experienced confusion around the two products. The decision to rebrand is tough, since it requires a significant investment to build awareness for something new. But as they continued to expand the product line further, the Freshdesk name couldn't support the evolving business and the confusion multiplied, with customers searching for Freshdesk CRM instead of the correct product name, Freshsales, and not recognizing that all these products were part of the same company. Jill eventually pitched and amassed support for the idea to rebrand the company to Freshworks.

Anita Moorthy, Former Head of International Marketing at Hearsay Systems, on International Expansion

Successful US startups that initially focus on the US market even-tually ask the question, should we go international? Most companies make the mistake of going international too early in their life cycle, because they're trying to raise money and it gives them a good story. But when they do it that way, they end up spreading themselves too thin.

One great approach that a company I worked used was to take the most experienced person in their current organization who knew the prod-ucts and the culture, had a great relationship with headquarters, and knew the customer and their challenges. They put this person in the role to grow internationally. The advantage was that this person had all the bridges back home to be able to convey the challenges and get the help that they needed. Since they had that bridge, they were able to move quickly in terms of iterat-ing on their current product and programs to address new market.

Some companies won't need to move and establish international operations for expansion. But if you do decide to make that leap, it is import-ant to understand a few things.

First of all, there's no such country as international. There's no country called International; there's no country called Europe. That mindset really comes to bite you back, because even just in Europe, every country is differ-ent. The UK is very different from Spain is very different from France. The countries are very different, not just in terms of the product requirements, potentially, but even culture-wise. For one, a dinner networking event is best; for others, a breakfast. They are all very nuanced.

Approach expansion on a country-by-country basis. Pick a few places that are the best market fit based on whatever it is that your product solves the pain for those markets, put a full unit together—a proper customer success person, an implementation person, a marketing person, and a prod-uct person. Make the investment in that country and really penetrate that market, and then move on.

Growing new segments will likely involve some internal coordination challenges and conflicts. Internal communication and collaboration will be critical to success. The idea should be that this cycle never really ends as long as your business continues to grow or you are looking for ways to continue to grow. Some combination of new products and new markets will focus your attention to start this process again. And while we agree that some efficiencies and having a supporting business infrastructure around you will help with some of these new directions, seldom—if ever—is it a cookie-cutter solution to add the new product or launch the new market.

As PayPal was expanding into new countries—while adding new products at the same time, to make this exponentially more complex—for speed and efficiency they adopted a playbook to launch country to country. France one month, Germany the next. Belgium, the Netherlands, and Luxembourg were combined into the BeNeLux launch the following month. To make this work, however, Todd had a 60-person customer success team to analyze and fix each launch for the few months after. France was retranslated from the Canadian-French first version; the value messaging was changed in Germany because they already had a successful banking solution like PayPal; the Belgians didn't really understand the website copy about buying baseball cards with PayPal since it wasn't culturally significant to them. As Anita Moorthy said above, each new product and each new market should be treated independently, with a team focused on making sure the relationship you want to have with your customer can be fully realized as you expand.

Moving Forward

At this point, you've built out your tools, content, and programs to support your customer journey, and you've invested in the teams and technology to support them. You're executing against your marketing plan and defined key performance indicators. You're measuring the results and evolving your programs. There are many directions you can go to take your business forward at this point. You can continue to invest in penetrating your core market(s), expand into new markets, and or build new products for your core market.

For some founders and leaders, this may be the end of the book for them. Building and running a successful business has been their aim, they now have a fully engaged marketing team to support the growth of the organization, and this is about the continued evolution of new products and markets.

Some may look at this as the beginning of the end for them in the organization as they think about transitioning out and on to something new or to think about an exit event for the organization. Or, as is often the case, the exit opportunity presents itself and requires the founder and team to investigate it. The following chapter will help founder and teams look at the various options for their next stage and how both communications and trusted resources can help navigate the exit stage.

7

EXIT THE BUSINESS

The looming question at this stage:

* How do I prepare for a successful exit?

This chapter will cover:

* Preparing for and managing communications throughout the exit stage
* Setting up the right communications team

E very beginning has an ending. At some point, the founder will come to the end of this thing that they created. And while there are only a few categories of what can happen—you fail, you IPO, you get acquired, or you leave—there are too many nuances to possibly cover here in this book. Either there is nothing left, you give control to someone else, or you leave.

There was common theme among the founders we talked with: no matter your outcome, the exit is tense. It is filled with emotion. It is challenging. We even heard from a few successful founders who stated that the successful exit was in some ways more challenging (monetarily, at least) than the others.

There are plenty of great books on exits and the nuance of the financing for those outcomes. What is often overlooked is this: just like few companies are an overnight success, few exits are successful without making smart decisions well before you enter that exit phase. Decisions you make at the earliest stages of your business greatly impact the outcome. This doesn't mean that you can't or shouldn't think about reacting to something in the market. It doesn't mean that even great plans may go sideways and the options are chosen *for* you. But, throughout this book, we discussed the importance of planning. Planning for your exit is just as important—if not more so—than planning on how to launch your first product.

Maha Ibrahim says:

> When a CEO tells me it's time to sell, it's time to sell. The CEO, at that point, is seeing the opportunity, and they're also assessing the future risk of the business. I will never tell a CEO that it's not a time to sell, if they are saying it's time to sell. Don't get me wrong, I will tell a company that it is time to exit, absolutely. What I won't do when a CEO tells me or a founder comes in and says it's time to exit, is tell them no.

No matter how this ends, how you communicate this is critical to closing off the past, addressing the present, and preparing for the future.

Communications Is Key and King

Communications is the primary concern at this stage, after determining the best decision to drive business outcomes. Nobody likes a surprise. The market, shareholders, stakeholders, employees, partners, customers—they especially dislike surprises. So no matter what your exit is, having a strategic communications plan is essential to mitigating risk and disruption, as well as fostering a successful landing for your exit plans.

There are three key communications considerations at this stage: trust, exit strategy and expertise, and audience.

Trust

You may have a communications person or team in place at this stage. You may have an external agency as well or consultants to help you with your press and media plans. This is a good time to evaluate whether you have the right players in place for your next steps.

Do you trust the people you have in this role? Regulatory issues aside, you have to absolutely trust your communications team for the lead-up events to an exit. They need to fully understand your desired outcomes and be privy to sensitive information and insight. If you don't trust them, you need to immediately think about bringing in another person or team to take over the responsibility. One easy litmus test is this: ask yourself—regardless of the person or teams role or title—if you would be comfortable having one of them sit in behind-closed-doors meetings about the exit and sharing *all* relevant insights and information about the exit and the timeline for that exit. If you are uncomfortable with this possibility, start looking for external help for this role. If you don't have full faith and trust in your resources, keeping them in the dark or not sharing relevant information will be folly; they will fail or miss expectations, and you will be frustrated and dissatisfied with the outcome.

Andy Cunningham says:

> I try to be very honest with my clients. I try to say, take a look at what the value is you can bring to the table, and if the value that you can bring would be better as a board member than it is as a CEO or as an operating person, you should think about that. So, I don't ever tell them what to do or anything; I just ask questions. Where do you think your skill level is? Where do you think your value add is at this point? How are you feeling about the rest of the team that you have? And really try to get them to think through their own emotions, and take it out

of the realm of emotion, and put it into the realm of intellectual thought.

Exit Strategy and Expertise

For every exit, there is a strategy. Start by asking if the team or individuals you have today have experience in the exit you are planning. Preparing for an IPO is vastly different and requires different steps than a founder exiting to pursue a next new idea. The moving pieces are unique to each circumstance, but they are complex and require a team that has had experience or near-experience to manage these steps. There are exceptions, but having people who can think though all the angles is important at this stage.

Ultimately, the founder and leadership team know the desired outcome and timeline, and the communications team needs to effectively execute a communications strategy to enable that outcome. They are there to execute strategy and to mitigate risks. This may be peppering the market with stories for months before the planned event, or it may mean a short-term blitz to address messages to the right audiences immediately before the announcement.

Audience

No matter what your exit strategy, there are separate and unique audiences that need to be messaged, if not downright managed, through the process. Employees, customers, partners, investors, stakeholders, and so on all have a different perspective on and relationship to the organization. Each needs to be communicated to; seldom does a cookie-cutter approach work here. The employee concerns are different from those of customers. A strong communications team will be able to develop a messaging strategy, timeline, and best platform to deliver the right message at the right time.

For many exits, the focus for a communications strategy is on market perception. However, your employees and customers can be great flag bearers for your message as well—if you will let them. Don't underestimate the skin in the game that many employees feel for the organization and their willingness to help carry the message forward. There are circumstances and nuances where this is not the case, but make sure you and your communications team are communicating with *all* of your audiences and make conscious, strategic choices on what you say and when you say it.

For example, an exec from one company that went public recently explained that they had to change how they reported their numbers internally, far ahead of the IPO, because of implications on how they would have to report the numbers to the street. They had to change what they shared and how often they shared it. They wanted to get employees used to these changes ahead of time. In addition, they had to educate employees on what they could and could not share on social media and what a quiet period meant, among other things.

Having a communications team that the leadership can put their full and complete trust into and who can help effectively steer the organization through the risks to a successful outcome is not an easy step for many leaders. This is why it is so key to have the right people in these roles.

Andy Cunningham on Transitions

The best situations are when the founder does have someone to talk to. This is when I feel like my role as marketing consultant moves from being marketing consultant to therapist. You're often in that position as a communication marketing consultant because you're dealing with founders typically who are very attached to their product or their company, and they are very emotional about it, so they really do need someone to talk it through with. When they're talking to a communication person like me, I have no agenda with them, but if they try to talk it through with their chief operating officer or their head of HR or their board, all of those people have agendas with the founder, and they will work to promote their agendas in their conversation with the founder. So it's not like a real therapy session, right? It's like you're talking to somebody and they're going to try to push what they think is the right thing to do. Whereas if you bring in someone like me who is an outside communication person who doesn't have a dog in the race, so to speak, I and people like me can actually provide a really great sounding board with no agenda at work, and that's a very valuable thing for a founder, to talk to somebody where the advice they're going to get is really to help the founder, not to promote an agenda that I might have with the business.

Communications has an important role during the full life of your company, but at your exit and other major inflection points in your organization, a great communications strategy dramatically increases your chances of success. LinkedIn had a near textbook example of how to communicate an exit with the acquisition by Microsoft. Both brands could have suffered with the transition (eBay and PayPal were famously at war with each other during their transition, and the employees never really gelled.) They communicated the value and the purpose as one team, with one message. Microsoft also knew where to add value and where to let LinkedIn be LinkedIn. There has been little disruption to their members, and both leadership teams have repeatedly touted the advantages of the move.

A recent AON/Hewett study showed that a little over half of highly engaged employees will slow down and you will get less out of them during an exit event. That means that—regardless of the outcome—some of your best people will underperform during these critical exit steps.

Neustar was going through an exit of sorts with the loss 50% of revenues and business after exiting a contract with the US government. A transition like that could be devastating for an organization. The company set upon an aggressive six-month program to address the revenue gap with existing products, launching into new markets and new countries, and through a thoughtful communications plan. Todd and his team spent the next six months with a continuous drip of communications internally with frequent updates and an executive roadshow, town halls, and lunch-and-learn events to hear directly from executives on a personal level. It was coordinated with months of active work with press and media to tell the story of the company and their plans for the future, yielding double-digit stories in top media outlets, and a coordinated war room during the event to address everything from customer questions to social media to reporters. Every executive was trained on talking points to articulate the vision and direction of the company going forward. The result: after losing 50% of revenue, the company lost only 3% of market value and recovered to have a banner year and a successful exit to private equity two years later because they developed a strong communications strategy and had the opportunity to execute it in the marketplace.

In many ways, how you communicate the event to all of your audiences—internal and external—can be just as important as the event itself. You are managing expectations and perceptions.

Having the Right People with You in the Boat

Common among founders who have gone through their exits is having the right people around you at the end. As Nikhil Raj put it:

> One of our board members is on the board not because he invested the most amount of money, but because we want him there. There is two decades of startup and deal experience in that one person. So anytime I have a question, I generally go straight to him. Then, as I learn more and get more comfortable... there's a particular point where you just listen to some advice and do it, versus listen to some advice, and decide whether you want to do it.

Andy Cunningham echoed something similar:

> It is a super hard challenge, because you are so connected to your company that you really can't even think anything but are emotionally charged about it. So, I think what founders need to... keep track of where their skills start and stop.

Nikhil Raj on Co-founders
Where we thought we made a really good decision was the co-founding thing. Picking people that you have such a deep relationship with was really the right thing to do in hindsight, thinking back. I'm like, oh my god, some of the tough discussions we've had. There's no way we would've come through it had we not known each other so deeply in the past. It's really important.

There's not only the regular decisions day to day, but also how do you allocate the capital? How much equity does each founder get? What do you do to make sure that the initial equity granted continues to sustain its value in the sense that the founder continues to create? Some people check out after a while, so how do you prevent that? How do you protect against that? How do you make sure that when somebody says they're going to do something, they actually do it operationally, because you're a founder, right? You get away with a lot of things because of the employees. But, you've got to have the responsibility to deliver on a lot of these commitments, and you want to be properly incentivized to do or not, so if you don't. Those are all really, really hard and difficult decisions…Okay you've found a good co-founder now how do you setup, structurally to make it successful?

What is important at this stage is to seek this counsel and use it effectively. We have heard and seen directly from more than a few leaders and founders that the concern around leaks or dissemination of information causes them to become less likely to seek counsel at this stage. Every situation is unique, and the management—not control—of information and the timing of that information requires some thoughtful planning and strategy. Hopefully, you have the right infrastructure of smart people and trusted confidants around you to help you make smart decisions about your exit.

Last Words

The exit is not the end. No matter how this ends for you, there is some next thing in store for you. There may be a beach vacation or a walk in the woods in between, but there is always something in store for the future. You may go back to the beginning and do it all over again or follow a new path. Serial entrepreneurs and founders who had at least one exit told us that the lessons learned from their experiences as founders stayed with them and helped steer and guide their life after.

Whatever happens, there will always be a next thing and another opportunity.

8
HIRING AND BUILDING

This chapter will cover:
- Considerations for hiring marketing talent

Judy Loehr recounts a story about referring a marketer to a startup:

> I had a company call and say, "We're looking for such a person, who can you recommend?" I referred somebody who I think is great. She went in there, and about six months later, the CEO called me again saying, "Yeah, we're looking for a new director of marketing." I asked what happened. "Oh, yeah. She didn't really cut it." And I thought that was interesting, because I've worked with her before. And this person wanted another referral. So, I thought of one more person. I'm not kidding you, six months later, they called and asked me for somebody else.

At this point, I refused to give them another name. I checked in with those two people, and the founders, CEO, and CTO were using marketing as the vehicle to sort of figure everything out. As a result, everyone was involved in every word of copy on every page of the website and the data sheet in every presentation. Now, each of those things is still important. I'm not saying the CEO should not be involved. He or she should be. But, each one was different, and they were using those as vehicles to try to figure out what was most important and what was relevant. And really, they didn't have any positioning to start with, hadn't gone through a lot of that thinking, and every word of copy on every little piece of collateral became an excruciating process.

So, what I say now is that if a company has gone through two directors of marketing or two heads of marketing within a year, it's probably not them; it's probably you. And it's time to look in the mirror.

What was surprising (but maybe should not have been surprising) was the number of times successful founders and business leaders shared the sentiment that your people—and not the product you build—are your most valuable asset. The idea makes sense and is not a new concept, but it was repeated again and again. Build a great team around you, or else there may some consequences.

It sounds like great advice, but there are a host of questions in there: What is "a great team"? What does that cost? How do I find them? Which order do I hire them in? Can I really build a culture, and does it matter? How should I interview them? What questions do I ask? Where do I find them, and what happens if they aren't right around the corner from me? What should their tenure with the organization be, and do I care if they move on?

We believe in the value of the team, and we will share some baseline insights to help founders and leaders as they build their organization across all five of our stages.

Founder Devin Redmond on Teams

There are lots of ideas, but execution is really what makes things happen, and execution happens not just by one person. Execution happens by having a good team and being able to take a team into a market, into an opportunity, and having that team be able to cover all the different scenarios they need... I've been fortunate to work with a lot of really gifted and talented people... people that you look at them and you go, "God these people are really smart, they're smarter than me. They're better than me."...Sometimes people have trouble saying that; I have no trouble saying that whatsoever.

My task in leading them is to make sure that we're balanced, that our team has the right set of skills and can work together effectively to the point where we can get all those things done, where we can look bigger than we actually are, where we can be good at telling our story and then delivering on our story at the same time. And now I think a lot of founders underestimate that part, again because they think about the idea and delivering the technology for the idea. But if you don't have the rest of those components and you're not all cohesive on the story and the go-to-market strategy and execution around everything from building to delivery to a customer, you start to run into a lot of those friction or points of angst where you know that it creates negative momentum for you and the rest of the team.

And so be thoughtful about that when you're building a team. Is this somebody who [has the right] skill set, or [is it] beyond their skill set? Is their persona really going to get us something that we need in the end? And I've been in organizations where you have that whole spectrum of really, really talented people but they're assertive, and they drive some of the tension in the organization, and that can be okay if it's balanced enough, but if there's no balance to that, then you run into those things that can bring you down over time.

Culture and Hiring

Brian Chesky, co-founder and CEO of Airbnb, expressed culture this way: "A company's culture is the foundation for future innovation. An entrepreneur's job is to build the foundation." The idea of culture is something of a buzzword and can tossed around almost recklessly by organizations that don't fully understand it.

Culture = Brand + Values + Purpose

Your brand is how anyone—inside or outside the company—perceives your organization.

Your values are what you use to help allow people to make decisions for the organization.

Your purpose is not just the product you create, but what you want your organization to achieve.

In this regard, culture is not some statement you put on the wall of your conference rooms; it has a pragmatic function to help you find and attract talent, partners, and customers. Your organization is going to develop a culture whether you want it to or not. And just like you won't leave your product's success in the market to chance without having strategy to deliver the product, similarly you should have a strategy to drive and build your culture—from that very first hire.

Brendan Browne thinks about culture a lot. As the VP of talent for LinkedIn, his job is to think about finding the best talent that adds to the culture and the success of LinkedIn.

> Culture's going to emerge no matter what. So if we start a company and then over six months we hire 10 people, a culture forms. If we don't do it with curation, intention, nurturing it, crafting it, who knows what it would be. It will run amuck, and we won't be able to make decisions as crisply or cohesively as we need to. A huge part of the founder's job is cultivating,

shaping, the culture and core values. You need a good product, and you need a good product/market fit, but it's not going to go anywhere unless you have an organization that is sound in terms of culture and values.

I think where most people miss when they underestimate the level of attention that goes into it or never really pay attention to it until it's too late. Focus on this the earlier the better. It is a very difficult thing to do—to change culture over 100 people or 1,000 people. it's probably the hardest thing to do in business.

The trick is to start thinking of culture in the correct terms, just like the idea of brand. If you think of the idea of your brand as something simple or tactical—like saying the brand is just things like my website or my logo—you miss the bigger picture. Culture is just like that. Thinking of culture merely in terms of employee happiness or everyone gets along misses the bigger picture. Culture has a pragmatic and practical role in your organization. And while this does take effort and requires someone to steer and guide it, it doesn't have to be a herculean effort.

Browne continues:

Begin the process of articulating and putting down on paper what you value and what that means in terms of culture. The culture's going to be reflective of the founder or founders at a certain level. So, the good news is a lot of that stuff is already there. You want the culture to mirror what you value, so this shouldn't be an artificial thing where you'll have to brainstorm and come up with some concocted or constructed axiom or set of language.

Your culture is your organization's ability to make decisions, address problems, and innovate into new directions. Your culture starts with your values. These values will give your employees and future employees guidance on how to make decisions and what you want this organization to be as it grows. As a founder, you may be able to be in every conversation for a time, but that doesn't scale. As you grow and entrust more and more people to share your vision but also evolve your vision, having these principles helps them make better decisions. This should be more than just the basic idea—like "act with integrity." What does that mean, and how do we act with integrity?

This is where your culture emerges and requires active participation from you and your leadership team. Use those values in your company meetings, say those words out loud, and exhibit those behaviors as part of who you are as a founder.

These ideas of brand and value and culture and purpose are interconnected. Not only do they define what this organization, company, product are going to look like, but they have a measurable impact on the people you will surround yourself for this journey.

Your purpose and values and what you stand for determine who is going to come on board with you for your journey. These ideas were echoed by Wendy Lea: "Good people are hard to find, and people have low tolerance of the bullshit. They're not going to put up with companies that don't have a purpose. They're not going to put up with companies that don't have good values. They're just not going to put up with it. It's not about the money. We see that at Uber, in spades, right?"

Your ability to attract that great talent comes from these core values, which build your culture and determine your company's trajectory. It is tempting to take a shortcut, just focusing on hiring the person you need for that role right now. Let this culture stuff go for later. This is a problem for another day—we need this role filled today. Especially if you—the founder—are doing the hiring, it may seem easy to control the types of talent you bring in and shape your company. However, as you grow and scale, others start making the hiring decisions. What if each organization starts to hire in their own image. Engineering hires their way, operations theirs. Finance is in a silo from product. Now what do you do when these groups have to work together? This isn't about function; this is about values and approach. What do those people stand for? Will they be able to collaborate and work toward common goals, or will those be at odds?

What has become more and more clear is that culture is not just some buzzword, but an active approach that leadership takes to help the organization and that provides them with a framework to make decisions. Just like building a product takes time and dedication and requires both strategy and execution, so too does the culture of the company. Left alone, it may perform well for a time, but it runs the risk of colliding with your values, or the needs of the market, or your customers. Culture is not some plaque on a wall or statue on a shelf—it is nurtured by the founder.

Your culture and brand are clearly communicated to potential hires in how you approach and manage the recruiting process. If brand is "what people say about you when you're not in the room," you want to consider everyone's experience with your company and your brand. Every interviewee, hired or not, has the potential to walk away saying positive or negative things about your brand. So consider your hiring process and experience carefully.

Todd had a recent experience with a high-growth-mode company. They were on a hiring spree to keep up with their demand in the market. After receiving a substantial funding round, the company looked to make some investments in their go-to-market team, specifically in marketing. An agency helped source some candidates, and one was made an offer. The team felt this was a great fit and was eager to move forward.

The CFO reneged on the offer and pulled it. He and the CEO had made a late-night decision to restructure their direction and pivot into a new space. These moves happen all the time in startup environments and are often necessary to keep the business moving forward, if not just to stay afloat. However, in this circumstance, the retraction of the offer at this stage was damaging to the candidate, the agency, and the team. Credibility was lost with the agency, who removed themselves from any future relationship with the company. The candidate had turned down another role in this process and was disheartened. The marketing team felt frustration on many levels.

While this may have felt like a good business decision, it had a ripple effect of negative impact on the perception of the organization, both internally and externally. We may at times feel like we are on an island, but our communities are small. Word travels fast, and what you do today is being echoed tomorrow with candidates for roles across your organization.

Your organization and your culture are the result of a series of decisions you make on how you treat and value you people, of the types of people you employ and the ones you keep out of your team.

Where to Start

When you first start out, you are the marketing team (and everything else), doing any and all marketing that needs to happen. When you need help and expertise, freelancers are a great way to supplement. They can polish your pitch deck, create a company logo, or anything else you need help with early on. The early chapters of this book can serve as a guide to get you started on what you need to be thinking about.

You'll likely make your first marketing hire around the Prove the Product stage. Unless you truly know how to reach your market early, you'll probably want that first hire to be a marketing generalist or a product marketer with a growth mindset who can create your early sales and marketing tools, run your first campaigns, and conduct experiments to begin to figure out your playbook.

As you move on to the Prove the Business stage and beyond, who you hire and how you build out your team will depend on your go-to-market approach and your playbook. Prioritize the most critical expertise you need to get the job done, the ones that will be core to your strategy, particularly the skills that can't easily be outsourced.

Hiring and Working Successfully with Freelancers, Consultants, and Agencies

We've all experienced failed consulting and agency engagements. There are many marketing agencies and consultants, and it can be difficult to assess their quality and whether they'll be right for you. The best way to find and vet an agency or consultant is through referrals. Have they done good work for someone you trust? Check out the work. Is it the same kind of work you need?

The keys to ensuring a successful engagement are:

1. **Set clear, realistic expectations and measures:** If you don't clearly and explicitly communicate your expectations, they aren't likely to be met. And be realistic. Your consultant isn't likely to magically pull perfect positioning out of a hat in a day or develop

a cheap campaign that builds significant brand awareness in just a few months.

2. **Set clear milestones for check-ins:** These periodic milestone reviews will allow you to review and course-correct quickly, before projects go too far down the wrong path.

3. **Stay involved:** They aren't likely to be successful in a vacuum. Either you or a capable member of your team needs to stay in close contact to know what they're working on, share your deep knowledge of the market, reset them if they start heading in the wrong direction, and make sure they get whatever they need from your organization.

Just like hiring a new employee, you should plan on it taking some time and energy to get consultants and freelancers started and manage them through their projects.

Finding and Vetting Marketing Talent

One of Wendy Lea's hallmarks is being able to find, recruit, and nurture great talent. But not every founder can be good at everything. Founders can be great visionaries but struggle to put that into practice. So much of building a great team around you is the approach to find them, vet them, and then win them over to you. Thinking through your talent strategy and then the practice of recruiting and vetting is challenging, but fortunately, it is a learned skill.

Like any other role, the first step is to map out your talent needs. This can be as simple as starting a table of all of your hires and your expectations for what that talent will cost you. While this may seem simplistic, it will help you at all stages—not just your earliest—to see where you are making investments in these valuable assets and how you are prioritizing parts of the business over others. Everything is a trade-off, a compromise. There is no unlimited pile of money and time—even if you have amazing financial backing, there are always limits and priorities.

When you have that big-picture strategy of the talent you want to hire, you can start to see how your organization is shaping up. Instead of just looking at the functional role, think about the strengths of people you bring in as well. An extreme example is strategy versus execution: If the people you bring in are all strategists, you will struggle executing your vision and spend all of your time talking about it. If they are all executors, you will struggle over every finite detail and miss the bigger picture. Dana Shaw thinks of this like interlocking pieces or a Rubik's cube. Over her past three companies and now working with other founders, she helps find the strengths in employees. "You want double-digit growth, you want to scale fast. Employees will move mountains for you if you know how to tap into them. Knowing their strengths and hiring for those will help you build that high-performing team you are looking for."

What appeared to be universal was asking good questions and having a few people interview for consistency. Consistency may seem simple enough as a concept, but when you are busy and that perfect candidate is front of you, it may be tempting to just say, "You're hired," and move on to your next issue. What was echoed by Brendan Browne and others was this idea of making sure your values and purpose are aligned to the interview process, interviewing beyond the function. This will require a few sets of eyes on them to help suss out the good from the bad—or the not-so-great fit.

Good questions are a bit harder. What good questions do you ask? The specific functional questions depend on the role, but the good questions we heard came in two flavors: our values and your values. Cara France in particular spends a great deal of time asking follow-up questions to every question.

> Sage has a value of growth and transformation. Everyone walks in and says, "It's really important to me that I can grow in this role." Well, somebody might go "Check!" We don't go check. We say, "Oh really? What does that mean to you?" "Well, it means that I'm going to get assignments that are challenging and, I'm going to keep growing." "Well, tell me more." It's continually digging to get at, when they say they want to grow, how does that align to what we mean about growth and transformation? When we talk about growth and transformation, it's uncomfortable. It's not easy. They might be talking about growth and transformation in a way of "I just want more opportunity and I expect to be promoted every 12 months." That's not what we mean by growth and transformation. So it's really digging in to understand whether

there's a behavioral alignment. That's the most important piece.

Wendy Lea tells her people, "Imagine you have the job and it's six months from now." She moves people into a place of them not wanting to being there, but being there for six months and what that looks like for them. She gets the conversation moving into an understanding of how the two sets of values may or may not coexist.

Like other roles, this is also where it is very important to understand the culture of your organization and your needs. If you're very metrics driven, then dig in with questions about prior projects, how they measured success, and where they've learned and changed course as a result. If you need someone who is really strong in messaging and positioning, have them walk you through the process they went through to define and validate it at their prior company.

No matter what approach you take and when you decide to hire a talent team to help you through this process, the recommended approach is very similar to what you do with your product, but your company is your product. Have a strategy, understand your value in that process, and invest your time and energy to understand the fit and alignment.

Assessing Marketing Talent

Erica Brescia knows that marketing isn't her core discipline.

> Hiring marketers in general is hard because they're marketers and they're really good at marketing themselves. Let's not over-look that. It is really hard if you're not yourself a great marketer to know what a great marketer looks like. And as with any role, there are some people that are exceptionally good, and there are a lot of people who are less good, and that is really challenging with marketing.

One of the pathways to success with hiring marketing people is one of the themes of this book—have a strong sense of what you are looking for and how that fits into the strategy. Erica, continued:

Everybody has a superpower, in my view. And you know a well-rounded marketer can do a lot of things well, but they usually have one thing that they do really well, and we put a lot of thought in our search around our business needs and the new business we just launched. Thinking about the role that way was really helpful. It led to a more successful outcome than some of our earlier searches, when we didn't have that level of clarity around where a person has great depth in order to help move the business forward.

If you have a strong sense of what you are trying to accomplish for your business, start thinking about the qualities you need in a marketer to help you meet or exceed those goals. This sounds simplistic—and it actually is. Think about the terms used to describe those people, and then look for those qualities in the resume or in the questions you ask. If you are in the Prove the Business stage, where you are iterating and testing, having someone with a test-and-learn mindset is key. They may be open to ambiguity and may be comfortable with risk. However, when you are well into Grow the Business, you may want to lean more on people who are more detail oriented, analytical, and execution focused. Very few people are just one or the other. Most marketers can move between these roles because—as marketers—most have had to adapt as the organization's needs have changed. But harkening back to Erica Brescia's statement, most marketers have a superpower and a comfort zone that is their strength.

Hiring marketers also ties back into your company purpose and values. If you are focused on customer, for instance, and really value the customer in your business, you want a marketer who is a steward of that idea and doesn't just see marketing as ones and zeros. Ask them questions about prior customer relationships or how they helped connect the company to customers and gave the customer a better experience. Whatever those values are should be articulated in the interview process, especially for these marketers. Marketers are front and center in your interactions with customers, the connection point between organizations like product and sales, and typically have strong ties and working relationships across the other organizations in your business. A misalignment in hiring marketing people that don't share your values, goals, and business purpose can be a costly fix—time and resources may be wasted along the way if you don't get this right.

Kevin Eyres on Starting with Why

The first real conversation is about why. I'm a big believer in Simon Sinek's work on start with why, and having the founder be able to articulate why the company is there. What is the vision? What is the mission of that being? And ensuring that they understand that you want people who are joining in that vision, that mission, because having that more of a heartfelt connection to what you're doing, is what's going to help bring the people all the way through. Clearly, when it comes down to the person themselves, the chemistry capability and fit, but it's helping the founders understand and be able to articulate why they're there, and then what it is about the person that they're looking for. And then down into the role. Having them articulate all of those different aspects and not just looking for "we need a magical solution" or this "rock star player" that's going to come in and do this. Take a step back whenever they're really eager to make that hire and start asking why.

The CMO Role

We heard several permutations on how organizations found their CMO. Executive search firms, internal hiring teams, from friends and their network, prior working relationships, up-leveling someone within the organization, or poaching from direct competitors—all of these work; all of these fail. One of the commonly held beliefs is that CMOs typically have an 18-month tenure at an organization. Part of this short tenure comes down to fit and timing.

Regarding fit, Jon Miller says it best:

> You see different flavors of marketing executives. At the highest level, there are generally three main focuses of strengths. One is traditionally the demand generation of revenue marketing side of things, the strength around creating lead and pipeline and so on. The second is around product, and that's your more classic Four

Ps side of marketing. What is the product? How are we positioning it? How are we pricing it, and so on? And then the third
is your sort of brand and corporate marketing. And that's both
more the creative side, the PR side, and the communication side
as well as some of those softer aspects of the emotional side of
marketing. You have those three main foci of strength. And again,
demand, product, and corporate marketing. One thing that's
really important to know is that I don't believe you're ever going
to find a unicorn CMO who is really strong at all three of these.
It's really critical to identify the area that's most important to you
and make sure you hire somebody who is great in that area.

And then, no, they're not going to be as great necessarily
in the other two, but in that case, as you think about building a
team over time, you'll need to compliment your marketing executive with people who are strong in the other areas. The reason
this is important for a startup is that when you're small, you're
not going to have that ability to really complement those other
areas with hiring out a big marketing team, and that makes it
even more important to really pick the CMO that's right for you.

As you are looking for that best CMO for your business, recognize that
person's core strength: product, demand, or corporate. How will that core
strengths help your business and how will you—together—fill those gaps in the
areas you need for your business? An example would be needing a strong product
marketing–focused person now, but realizing you need to move into a more
demand and growth mode later. How will you support your CMO with the
demand and growth aspects later?

Stacey Epstein on Assessing Marketing Success
*Every department in the company should be focused on driving revenue,
especially marketing. Marketing should be measured on revenue, and that
takes sales and marketing alignment.*

One of the ways I force that into the thinking of the company is by having a demand generation model. The model starts with the bookings target. From the bookings target you work down the spreadsheet: "Well, how much pipeline do I need to hit that bookings target? How many leads do I need to create that much pipeline?" You look at conversion rates, and that is a process that's done with sales and marketing together.

It's a way to force through the organization, the marketing organization, "We're here to generate bookings, not leads, not even pipeline, but bookings." It forces it into the minds of the marketers.

I always judged my team partially as a CMO based on "Is the sales team coming to me and telling me that Kathryn's doing an awesome job for them?" Because that's what I want to know. I don't want to know that she threw a great event, or she did a great campaign. I want to know that she helped someone close a deal. It's a philosophy in the organization.

At certain stages of your specific startup, bookings or revenue may not be the right measure. Whatever your overriding goals are, be clear about them for yourself and your team and use metrics to align and focus your marketing team.

When CMOs Fail

THIS BABY HAS A LONGER TENURE THAN MOST CMOs

What we have seen time and again—from our direct networks or covered in business media—is the CMO ousted after a short tenure because of lack of clarity about what you really need or misaligned or changing expectations. It is worth mentioning that this misalignment is absolutely a two-way street. Marketers—especially ones in that top slot—need to know their strengths and weaknesses, be clear about them, and know how to address those as the business grows.

The second reason for the shortened or poor fit for the business is timing. As Jon Miller mentioned, the CMO has a core strength and gaps in other areas. Those gaps can be filled with additional talent that ebbs and flows with the business and your growth. The organization can bring on new employees, hire agencies or consultants, or use small teams in the company to fill those gaps. This works when the marketing leader has the right core skills and experience that the business needs but lacks depth in some specific channels or domains.

The challenge for companies that hire a CMO too early, before they know enough, before they truly understand their business, target market, and go-to-market strategy, is they end up with a CMO who lacks the expertise and capability to help them get where they need to go. When your company is moving through these stages of proving and growing, you may find that what you need changes pretty quickly. Hiring a CMO may mean that this person fits really well at one stage, but is not aligned at a later stage. This causes those shortened tenures. Therefore, when you think about getting that CMO-level talent in the organization, address those questions about growth, gaps in talent, and how to address those over time.

It is challenging to know exactly what you need in the future or the resources you may have at your disposal to address those needs. And exactly when to bring them on may not be crystal clear. This is where you network of mentors and advisors is so critically helpful. Your business goals and your values help to establish both the talent of the person as well as the fit. Having direct questions and even assessing the candidates talent to determine their awareness of their strengths and weaknesses will help. And then asking yourself why—why now, and why do we need this role?—are ways to start finding that next right talent.

CMO Success

Not all CMOs end in failure, though success may not always look the same. There are CMOs who have been leading their organizations—usually enterprise companies—for over a decade. But a CMO may also step in for 18 months or two years to help get your organization over a major hurdle or through a big milestone. After that point, the organization may require a different skill set in that role to see it through the next phase. It all comes down to the skill set aligning to the dynamically changing needs of the business.

A good CMO not only accomplishes their major marketing objective—growth, branding, IPO, acquisition, and so on—but they can also help establish the culture of the marketing organization and the overall company. Frequently, the CMO is a key evangelist for the organization—internally and externally. Their role as that lead marketer gives them a stage—quite literally—to espouse the value of the organization across a wide array of audiences.

As you consider CMO candidates and evaluate what is right for your organization—both today and tomorrow—look at both the inspirational and aspirational. Think about who you want representing you externally, in the marketplace as well as internally, celebrating accomplishments and rallying employees when times are tough. It may be easy to dismiss this as a secondary soft skill, but a CMO who can rally a crowd and win over audiences has tremendous value no matter what the growth stage of your company.

As Tony Hsieh, CEO of Zappos, said, "We believe that it's really important to come up with core values that you can commit to. And by commit, we mean that you're willing to hire and fire based on them. If you're willing to do that, then you're well on your way to building a company culture that is in line with the brand you want to build."

9
CONCLUSION

Prove,

Prove,

Prove,

Grow, and

Exit

When we think about the journey of a founder, that is it:

1. Prove the idea
2. Prove the product
3. Prove the business
4. Grow the business
5. Exit the business

As we've gone on this journey ourselves and talked with others who have as well, we found those five key steps in every story. What was core to each person's journey were the fundamental questions for those stages. There are other great questions at each stage, but these were the essential questions each founder struggled with.

Does My Idea Have a Customer?

You have this amazing idea, but does your idea solve a problem that people truly care about, or is it a solution in search of a problem? Plenty of those great ideas have passion and energy behind them but never materialize. Often it has nothing to do with the product or the execution of building it, but everything to do with the fit in the marketplace. "Who are my buyers?" and "What do they want?" are two questions that if not asked and addressed will sink even the coolest of ideas.

In the rush to build and move forward, missing the vital step of identifying your market and then testing to see how sample customers react makes your chances of success exponentially less likely.

How Do I Fit the First Puzzle Pieces Together?

Having a longer-term vision for your product and thinking toward the horizon is good. But the proven path toward success is finding your right fit in the marketplace and then winning with a small, targeted group. Before the money, which is certainly important, think of this as having a small—even cultish—group of loyal customers who garner tremendous value from your products. You validate your value in the marketplace and develop loyal customers who become champions and advisors for future growth and direction.

Should I Bet It All on Red?

Once you have an idea of what your product is and how it connects with your loyal customers, it is tempting to go all in or place big bets in one or two areas. A few companies have done this and been successful. These tend to be showcased in the business journals. Big bets at this stage more often fail and lead to two things: you miss out on a great growth opportunity, and you have squandered your resources and now don't have them to scale and grow your business.

Placing small bets and truly understanding where your customers are, what they want to buy, and how to connect with them will highlight a true roadmap to them and provide a plan to use your limited resources wisely.

When Should I Take a Big Risk?

Once you have a sense of who and where your customers are and you know how to reach them, what seemed like a big bet—a big risk—at prior times will actually be a safe bet. You can go big on a program or campaign or you can make big investments because you know where the payoff will be and what your return on that investment will look like.

How Do I Exit Gracefully?

There is an exit in your future. It may be inconceivable, or you may be racing toward it, but there comes a time when you know it is time to move on. Exits vary wildly, but what was consistent across our successful experiences and key leaders who have led them was the communication strategy for that exit. Knowing what to say and when to say it—and having trusted people around you to help you figure that out—was the key to the moving from the exit and on toward your next beginning.

Closing Thoughts

In many ways, you probably have to be crazy to launch a new business. But frankly, that is what we love about you. Jill and Todd have lived through the ups and downs of startups. This book itself has been an entrepreneurial endeavor using the principles of the book, from pitching the investors (publisher), to crafting our product and testing it with the market, to launching it and marketing it, and then reacting to our customers (you) as it lives in the market.

We wrote this book to help you navigate your big idea toward success. The goal and idea of success is your own, but we look for this to be a guide that helps you through every step of your journey.

Through the process of writing this book, more than anything, we enjoyed having the opportunity to talk with and learn from so many experts. We took something away from each and every one and through the process evolved our thinking.

Your role as a founder and as a Swiss army knife for the organization is challenging. We hope this book serves as a reference that can offer new guidance as your organization grows and matures. We hope that your perspective changes as ours has, and that it brings you success—however you define it.

As the old saying goes, success comes from doing the common thing uncommonly well. We are happy we can help you on your journey of being uncommon.

Acknowledgments

We have been fortunate to have a team of experts, supporters, friendly smiles, and genuinely interested people who have helped make this book a reality.

We dedicated the book to our families, and we need to further acknowledge them here. Long nights, weekends, and missed opportunities went into this work. You were there for us every step of the way. Our love and gratitude is immeasurable. Without you, this would not have been possible.

Alan Berkson: This really is all your fault.

The many voices that contributed to this book through interviews and discussions: You validated the known and helped us uncover the unknown. This work was written by two authors and, thanks to you, includes many more decades worth of wisdom. We want to thank our many people who contributed their stories and experience to this book:

Erica Brescia, Co-founder and Chief Operating Officer, Bitnami

Brendan Browne, VP of Global Talent Acquisition, LinkedIn

Emilia Chagas, CEO, Contentools.com

Kate Bradley Chernis, Founder and CEO, Lately

Mei Chuong, Co-founder and COO, Zeuss Technologies, Inc.

Bruce Cleveland, Founder and GP, Wildcat Venture Partners, and author of *Traversing the Traction Gap*

Andy Cunningham, Founder and President, Cunningham Collective

Meredith Dunn, VP Styling and Client Experience, Stitch Fix

Nancy Duarte, CEO, Duarte, Inc., and best-selling author

Christina Ellwood, CMO and entrepreneur

Stacey Epstein, CEO, Zinc, and former CMO, SuccessFactors and ServiceMax

Kevin Eyres, Executive Coach and Hoffman Teacher, Conscious Leadership

Cara France, CEO, Sage Group

Folia Grace, VP of Marketing, Talkdesk

Paul Greenberg, Managing Principal, The 56 Group, LLC

Manish Gupta, CMO, Redis Labs

Lea Hickman, Partner, Silicon Valley Product Group

Carter Hostelley, CEO and Founder, Leadtail

Maha Ibrahim, General Partner, Canaan Partners

Cheryl Kellond, Co-founder and CEO, Apostrophe, Inc.

Bryan Kramer, CEO, Purematter, and bestselling author

Courtney Kramer, Executive Creative Director, Purematter

Erik Larson, CEO and Founder, Cloverpop

Wendy Lea, Board of Directors, Techstars, and Former CEO, Cintrifuse

Rebecca Lieb, Analyst and Founding Partner, Kaleido Insights

Judy Loehr, Enterprise SaaS Investor, Advisor, and former acting CMO for multiple SaaS startups

Bill Macaitis, CEO, Macaitis Advisory, and former CMO, Slack and Zendesk

Steve Mankoff, General Partner, TDF Ventures

Meera Mehta, VP of Marketing, InMobi

Jon Miller, CEO and Founder, Engagio, and Co-founder of Marketo

Margaret Molloy, Global CMO, Siegel+Gale

Anita Moorthy, former Head of International Marketing, Hearsay Systems

Arjun Moorthy, CEO, OwlFactor

Mike Moran, President, Mike Moran Group

Anita Pandey, Startup Marketing Leader

Dimitry Pavlov, Founder, CEO, Stitched Insights

Greg Powell, Head of Brand and Product Marketing, Fundbox

Nikhil Raj, Startup Founder, Investor, Advisor

Devin Redmond, Co-founder and CEO, Theta Lake, Inc.

David Rich, SVP, Client Services, World Expo, and Olympic Activations, George P. Johnson Experience Marketing

Ian Roncoroni, Co-Founder and CEO, Next Caller

Jason Saffran, CEO, The Lost Tribe

Dale Sakai, Co-Founder, Obo

Dana Shaw-Arimoto, Founder/CEO, Phoenix5;; LLC owner of Stop Settling®: Settle Smart

Will Staney, Founder and CEO, Proactive Talent

Blake Tablak, VP, Sales, Workiva, Inc.

Anand Thacker, Serial Entrepreneur and Startup Investment Advisor

Lauren Vaccarello, VP of Marketing and Customer Engagement, Box

Villy Wang, TED Speaker, Founder, CEO, and President, BAYCAT

Casey Winters, Scaling and Growth Advisor, Casey Accidental

Feedback is a gift. Our pre-readers each spent many hours poring through our unformatted error-prone drafts and shared thoughtful feedback that helped shaped this book: Alan Berkson, Monica Brady-Myerov, Sameer Goel, Carter Hostelley, Meera Mehta, Vijai Mohan, Anita Moorthy, Arjun Moorthy, and Greg Powell.

As with most good entrepreneurial efforts, we broke new ground but needed someone who had already paved their own way to show us the trail. Bryan Kramer was that voice in the wilderness saying "this way" when we needed it— which was often.

Ever meet someone and think, *I wish I could live in their head for even a day?* Carter Hostelley is Todd's "I want to be you when I grow up" person. Jill just thinks the world of him. He helped us unlock some doors and—even better— keep a few shut.

Writing a book while working at a startup full time is folly. Erik Larson and the whole Cloverpop team have been amazing coworkers, providing great examples of how to do things right and being incredibly supportive throughout the writing process.

Meera Mehta and the rest of Jill's Sloan marketing friends provided some of the inspiration for this book and have been an invaluable resource throughout.

Not every idea made the book, but, in the end, it had little to do with the value of the effort. Dr. Aaron Vanderhoof was one of those who produced a great chapter, on the health of the leader, that ultimately did not make the book.

Some people just set your life in the right direction. If you are lucky, you have a group of them that meet on a Saturday morning, and if you are lucky, you can be a part of a circle of friends whose guidance is felt decades later. Thank you Frank Eagan and the Rock Cola Gang.

Many, many more wonderful friends supported us in various ways throughout, hosting playdates while we wrote, talking through ideas, recommending more people to interview, and generally keeping us sane.

Lori Paximadis, our incredible editor, took what was raw and made it real. Lori weaved two voices into one and led our reader on a journey when we meandered. You are more than we had ever hoped for.

David Hancock and the team at Morgan James: From that first phone call and through the tense moments in between, you brought discipline, joy, and a kickass greeting for every phone call. We could not have done this without you.

Dave Kirby and the marketing team took our musings, our vision, and our random thoughts and turned them into something amazing. We love when someone can start to finish your thoughts for you.

We owe much to illustrator Henry Limargo and designer Miladinka "Mella" Milic, who added color and pictures to our words. It added great music to our lyrics.

Everybody who said no, you made us try a little harder and get a little more creative in our approach. Everybody who said yes, you made it a little easier and helped us make it even better.

And all of our mentors, colleagues, and everyone who taught us everything we know throughout our careers—we don't have enough pages to include all your names, but you're all in here.

There is always the risk of missing someone—for anyone who is not directly mentioned here, please accept our apologies and know the mistake—like all the mistakes we make—are on us and not a reflection of your impact and value.

Last, every entrepreneur we have worked with, interviewed, and gotten to know over the years, you all in here in some way. We have been inspired by and learned from all of you and look forward to bringing those lessons to the next wave as they follow in your footsteps.

CPSIA information can be obtained
at www.ICGtesting.com
Printed in the USA
LVHW110332230119
604872LV00001B/5/P

9 781642 791259